Monsters and Maniacs

True Tales of Mystery and Horror

John Harker

Some names, locations, and similar identifying details have been changed to protect the identities of the individuals who were either witnesses to or victims of these phenomena.

Table of Contents

Introduction

"There are more things in heaven and earth, Horatio,
Than are dreamt of in your philosophy."

– William Shakespeare, *Hamlet*

One of life's blessings is coming into contact with people who enrich us with their kind words, good deeds, and enviable examples. Sometimes it's not a person, per se, but another type of sentient creature—a beloved pet, a departed spirit, or an angelic being, for example—that crosses our path and keeps us from harm, raises us up, or simply soothes us with their presence.

But sometimes we cross paths with a different type of being, one that is neither heroic, humane, nor even human. Their deeds are despicable, their words are deceitful, and their presence is anything but comforting. They seek not to inspire and build, but to terrorize and destroy. They walk along our streets, creep around our houses, hide in our closets, and hover over our heads. They are the monsters and maniacs of our world.

This book offers a look into that disturbing world. Its purpose is not to provide answers to mysteries that can't be solved or to wax philosophically about mankind's place in the universe. It is simply to make aware that beneath the light and cheery trappings of our everyday, normal lives, there exists a dark underbelly of strange creatures, evil entities, and homicidal humans.

I hope these accounts succeed in their task to inform, enthrall, and entertain. But I also hope they help you see your environment with unclouded eyes and a discerning mind. Both are needed to navigate the dangerous world we share with our seen and unseen adversaries.

There are fiends in our midst; of this, there is no doubt. They may reside in your neighbor's house. They may *be* your neighbors. They could surprise you on a dark country road. Attack you in your bed. Or knock on your door late at night.

Be on the lookout. Be prepared. But also take comfort in this:

No, there isn't a monster behind every door.

Just every other one.

CHAPTER 1

The Blood Drinker

The full moon lit up the macabre scene as well as any theater lights could ever illuminate a stage. But the act that was playing out was far from make-believe. In a secluded clearing amidst a dank, shadowy forest, the assembled cast swayed and chanted before their director, who also played the starring role. Adorned in a satiny black robe, a wolf's mask hiding her face, the High Priestess held aloft a silver chalice filled with blood.

"Hail, Satan!" the woman exclaimed.

"Hail, Satan," her cohorts bayed, their dark-hooded robes revealing no identities nor offering any individualities, save those known only to their dark lords.

The woman drank deeply from the cup, then placed it down upon the stolen gravestone that was being used as an altar. She reached under the slab and pulled from a box a struggling rooster. With one hand she held the agitated bird around its neck while with the other she grabbed a large jewel-encrusted dagger. Looking out to her enraptured audience, she invited them to come closer. Then, raising the dagger high in the air, she cried out, "Ave Satanas!" and drove the dagger deep into the screeching rooster. Again and again, she stabbed at the bird. When finally all life had leaked from its brutalized body, she tossed aside the knife and held the animal in two hands.

"Come, lovely servants of Satan. Come and be anointed with the sacrificial blood."

She raised the bleeding animal up high and shook it vigorously from side to side, its fresh, warm blood spraying all within reach. Fortified by their unholy christening, the gathered began to quiver and murmur. Soon their movements became frenzied, their sounds animalistic, as they tore off their robes and fell upon each other in debauchery.

The woman smiled. The power she wielded was overwhelming at times. No other feeling on earth had ever satisfied her as much. She took the chalice and took another deep drink. Then she loosened the tie on her robe, let the garment drop, and walked into the mass of undulating bodies.

Jessica thirsted for power from an early age. While other teenage girls in the late 1960s were wearing flowers and feeling groovy, Jessica was searching for superiority and dominance. This deep desire, coupled with a long-held fascination with morbidity and death, led her quite naturally to the occult. Seduced by its promise of hidden knowledge and magical powers, Jessica threw herself into the study of the dark arts, determined to master its many mysteries. In short time, she grew adept in the basics of astrology, spells, and divination, but what she really wanted was the ability to "conjure something up." She soon got her chance when her boyfriend, Carl, unexpectedly broke up with her.

Believing she could get him back with the help of the spirit world, Jessica went straight to the top and invoked the Archfiend himself, Satan, to heed her request. She then waited all night for a remorseful visit or a contrite phone call from Carl. When it was apparent nothing like that was going to happen, Jessica decided to go to bed, disappointed but determined to try again the next day. As she got ready to turn in, something caught her eye in the mirror above her dresser. A strange mist was forming in the glass. She peered closer and was surprised to see not her own reflection but the face of a half-human, half-wolf creature slowly manifesting from out of the mist. Horrified, she tried to turn away, but the creature's glowing eyes and penetrating gaze held her in place for what seemed an eternity. Then slowly the image began to blur and fade until Jessica was left staring at her own whitened and sweat-drenched face.

Though she looked weak and afraid, she felt anything but. She felt energized, strong, and . . .bloodthirsty. An overwhelming urge to kill something, anything, rushed through her. The sensation was frightening and exhilarating at the same time. If someone had been there with her, she had no doubt she would have attacked them with an animal-like ferocity. As the feeling slowly started to fade, she tried to summon back the figure in the mirror. She knew instinctively that it was the source of her bloodlust and the accompanying sense of invincibility. But as much as she tried, the wolf creature did not reappear.

As she ruminated over things during the next few days, Jessica came to believe that her boyfriend's best friend, Jarod, was responsible for their breakup. She had never particularly liked Jarod anyway—he was a loser and a bore, in Jessica's opinion—but now she felt such an intense hatred for him that she became obsessed with the irrational yet irresistible idea of killing him. She turned to the wolf creature for help.

That evening, Jessica gazed into her mirror and, picturing Jarod in her mind with a hate so intense it made her shake, invoked the creature she had seen the other night. To her astonishment and delight, it appeared as it had before, and Jessica wasted no time asking for its help. The wolf *demon*, its nature no longer in doubt, then taught Jessica an arcane voodoo ritual. She was instructed to fill a bucket with water and concentrate intensely until she could see Jarod's face appear on the surface of the water. Then she was to take a large knife and stab at the image repeatedly until the water turned to blood. That would be the sign that Jarod would die.

Though Jessica performed the ritual over and over that night, conjuring Jarod's face and stabbing at it viciously, the water never turned to blood. She returned the next night to try again, with the added promise to her demon master that she would kill herself if the ritual worked and Jarod died. But at the very moment she made clear her suicidal intent, the wolf demon appeared and demanded that she stop and forget all about Jarod *and* her boyfriend. There were better things for her to do in the service of Satan now that she had proven her loyalty. Jessica didn't argue. In fact, she was thrilled with her new-found status in Satan's inner circle. Strangely, the mind-numbing hatred she had felt for Jarod just moments before was suddenly gone. He and Carl both were nothing but fading memories in her head now. For Jessica, that made life much easier.

With renewed vigor, she immersed herself in the study and practice of black magic, luxuriating in her newly granted freedom and understanding. She didn't need other people in her life to make her happy; she could obtain anything she needed or desired from the magical dark realm in which she was now a player. In her ongoing quest for knowledge and power, she invited multiple demons to enter her body, convinced that they could help her connect to a higher dimension, reach an altered state of consciousness, or, in simple terms, become superhuman. As she soon learned, the demons were having an effect on her, but a shockingly different one than she was expecting.

On a beach vacation with a friend, Jessica slipped away one night to explore on her own. As she walked through the streets of the old Cape Cod village, she pulled a blanket around her shoulders tightly like a cape to ward off the chilly air. Eventually she found herself in an old, historic cemetery. Guided by the light of an almost-full moon, Jessica wound her way through the rows of deteriorating headstones while feeling nearly giddy. It was as if she belonged here, she thought bemusedly. There was an energy present, an unseen force stirring something up within her, a need, a desire—

She shivered vigorously, her attention suddenly back upon her immediate surroundings and the encroaching cold. She made her way out of the cemetery and sat upon a low stone wall that bordered the burial site. She wanted just a few minutes to consider what had happened to her back at the graves. Her thoughts were interrupted, though, when a young man in his early twenties, who had clearly been drinking, ambled over and asked if he could sit next to her. Jessica tried to ignore him, but he sat down anyway and engaged her in a friendly, albeit mostly one-sided, conversation. After a short time, Jessica edged nearer to him, threw her blanket around the two of them, and leaned in close. Pleased that his charms seem to have worked, the man leaned in to meet her kiss. But a kiss was not what Jessica had in mind. With surprising alacrity, she pulled his head down, bit into his exposed neck, and slurped up the resultant flowing blood. Now fully sober, the man yelled out and jerked away. Though he easily outweighed her, something in Jessica's eyes made him turn and run off into the night with his hand pressed to his neck. Jessica watched as the terrified stranger fled from her. She reached up to wipe the dripping blood from her mouth and looked down at her crimson hands. She couldn't believe what she had done. Was she going insane? Or was it something else, something that was acting through her?

Whatever the cause, Jessica didn't let it bother her for too long. From her studies in the occult, she knew others shared her proclivities, and she felt now was the time to seek them out. She joined a local satanic coven and, with the assistance of her demon guides and her own adroitness, she quickly rose in the ranks to high priestess. The coven's rituals routinely involved the sacrifice of animals, which the grisly group carried out in deserted sand pits in the woods. Jessica soon discovered, however, that the blood of animals wasn't enough to satisfy her lust. She started picking up young men and leading them to the sand pits, where she would work them into a sexual frenzy before sinking her teeth into their shoulders or necks and lapping up the blood. The bites were never serious enough to warrant medical aid but were enough to satisfy her cravings. At times, the urge was so strong that she couldn't wait for a partner and drank her own blood instead.

Sharing Jessica's unholy appetite was her friend Karen, a member of the coven and fellow devotee of the dark arts. Many times when they were together, Jessica and Karen would draw blood from their arms with hypodermic needles and mix it with wine to satisfy their ghoulish cravings. Jessica had to stop this practice eventually, though, as her arm became so infected that at one point doctors thought it might have to be amputated.

When they weren't drinking their own or each other's blood, Jessica and Karen devoted themselves to other activities in service of their satanic lord. They stole religious items from churches, contaminated holy water, desecrated Catholic communion wafers, burned Bibles, and kidnapped pets to be used for sacrifices at their black masses. Jessica also felt increasingly drawn to cemeteries and, much like her vacation experience, found herself wandering around them at night, reveling in the mysterious dark energies that rippled through her body as she walked among the dead. One time when she was with Karen on one of these midnight excursions, the two even talked about digging up a body.

Though she was, for the most part, completely enamored with her chosen lifestyle, Jessica did experience moments of doubt from time to time. How, she wondered, could any sane person enjoy the ugly, unnatural things she did? Increasingly, she also began seeing the face of the wolf demon in other people's faces. Sometimes it occurred in strangers she passed on the street. Other times it was in people she knew. It manifested most often in her friend Karen. It was on one such occasion with Karen that Jessica was forced to see evil in its undisguised form.

The Christian holy day of Candlemas was nearing, and the two women planned to defile it in the most heinous way possible: with a human sacrifice to Satan. Their first thought was to kidnap a baby for the abominable act, but then Karen came up with a different plan. She had hated her father for a very long time, and she told Jessica that he was the one they should kill. She would trick him into coming to the ritual site, she said, and once there she would stab him in the back, over and over again until his insides spilled out, and then they could feast upon his flesh and organs. Jessica stared at her friend in horror. Though she herself had committed many atrocious acts, the frenzied glee that Karen displayed while describing the barbaric murder of her father sent chills throughout her body. Her fear grew greater when Karen's face, already twisted and ugly with rage, morphed into the contorted and grotesque visage of the wolf demon. When it focused its piercing, malevolent eyes upon Jessica, primal terror kicked in and sent Jessica running from Karen's apartment.

Feeling like a veil had been lifted from her eyes, Jessica vowed to never see Karen again and to cut all ties with her satanic sect and its profane rites. But she also knew that she needed help to walk away completely. The demons inside her were too strong and would never allow her to reject them without a fight. She also knew she was a slave to her bloodlust and that the strength of the coven would call to her soon. She reached out to paranormal investigators Ed and Lorraine Warren, whom she had heard about in the local news, and told them her story. They listened with sympathy and prayed over her, and then told her bluntly: Leaving would not be easy. She had willingly given herself over to evil so completely, and for so long, that it would require a major shift in lifestyle and belief to break that bond. She would need to move far away, refrain from all occult practices, and renounce all ties to evil. Jessica cast her eyes down and cried.

As she feared it would, the challenge proved too great for Jessica. In two weeks' time, she was back with the coven. Karen no longer talked about killing her father, but Jessica knew it was just a matter of time before murderous intent became reality for one or more of the coven members. She would deal with that when the time came. For now, all that mattered was the ritual taking place. Bathed in moonlight, the devil's disciples gathered around her, their chanting voices mingled in vile worship at the sand pits. Soon flutes, tambourines, and drums started up, providing a background of cacophonous noise to accompany the participants' increasingly salacious dancing. As they swayed and jerked to the harsh, discordant notes, their naked bodies gleaming with sweat, the worshippers passed around a jug of witches' brew: wine mixed with devil's nettle, wormwood, nightshade, laurel leaves, absinthe, morning glory seeds . . . and blood.

For one brief moment, a lucid thought flashed through Jessica's mind before she gave herself up to the rapturous waves of Bacchanalian euphoria. It was the memory of the note she had written for the Warrens just that morning.

Please help me! I'm into black magic again and so deep
I'm afraid I'll never get out. Our lord wants humans now,
no more animals. I don't want to, but I can't resist! I saw

the wolf again. He told me I only have a short time to live. What do I do? I don't want to die!

As quickly as it came, the memory withdrew. As it faded, she faintly recalled the despondency that drove her to write it. It seemed so silly now. What had she been thinking?

Nothing could separate her from the bloodlust of Satan.

Nothing.

* * *

After sending that note to the Warrens, Jessica never contacted them again. Whether she stayed with the coven or was finally able to escape her demons is unknown. It is also unknown if the coven ever carried out any human sacrifices.

What is certain is that bloodlust, at least one variation of it, is a real thing. The variety called hematolagnia is defined as: *A sexual fetish for blood which evokes arousal when present on the fetishist's sexual partner, especially if nude. It is often accompanied by licking or drinking blood through bloodletting or biting.*

According to an article in the BBC publication *Science Focus*, there are three other concepts of bloodlust that are popular in thought but less well-defined or provable by evidence.

1. The magical belief that blood is a medium that brings us into contact with a supernatural world and which demons can use to drive us to insanity.
2. The evolutionary idea that bloodlust is a prehistoric remnant of our struggle for survival in a violent past.
3. The aesthetic view that pleasure can be derived from what is actually repugnant and fearful.

Jessica's bloodlust was more than a belief, an idea, or a view. For her, it was a diabolical compulsion, a damnable desire—a hellish reality.

CHAPTER 2

The Shadow Men

Kristen called him The Dark Man on the Stairs because that's where he always appeared. At night when Kristen was alone—she was always alone when it happened—the tall shadow figure would emerge on the lower landing of the staircase and silently descend down the steps. Then it would turn left toward the kitchen, take a few steps, and "vaporize," as Kristen recalled. This same scenario played out multiple times over 18 months in a house Kristen and her children had moved into shortly after her divorce. The first time the apparition appeared, Kristen thought, "Did I just see what I thought I saw?" What she thought she saw was the black shadow of a man in a suit and hat. Even though no distinctive features were visible other than the outline of the figure, Kristen was certain it was a man and that he was dressed like someone from a 1930s black-and-white movie. She admitted that while she was "creeped out," she wasn't really frightened. The apparition didn't appear threatening, and over the next year and a half, she got used to seeing it go on its nightly jaunt from the stairs to the kitchen. Her feelings toward her uninvited houseguest changed, however, when one night she heard her five-year-old son, who had been sleeping in an upstairs bedroom, screaming hysterically. She burst into his room and saw her frightened son sitting up in bed, waving his hands around and yelling, "Get rid of them, Mama. All these people! Make them go away!" Though Kristen saw nothing out of the ordinary, the incident upset her enough to move her family out of the house within weeks. Thankfully, neither the Dark Man nor his friends followed her.

The Dark Man is just one of many names given to a class of enigmatic and menacing entities known collectively in modern jargon as "shadow people." These blacker-than-black humanoid figures usually, but not always, appear in the nighttime hours and are often seen in a viewer's peripheral vision, a fleeting glimpse that quickly disappears when looked at face-on. At other times, they appear more clearly, sitting in a corner, perhaps, or standing at the end of a bed, staring at the occupant. Or, as in Kristen's case, walking from one area to another.

Sometimes, like the Dark Man, they are seen wearing a 1930s-style fedora; at other times a hood like a monk's cowl covers their head. They can appear tall and willowy, or child-sized and plump. Some walk, some sit, some crawl. Some are seen only in the backgrounds of photographs or in mirrors. At other times, they first appear as dark outlines on a wall that then detach and move about. While usually their silhouettes are recognizably human, at times the shadows appear as shapeless blobs or swirls of smoke, sometimes with tendrils or claw-tipped arms projecting outward. They have no discernible mouths, noses, or facial expressions, although on rare occasions they have been seen with glowing red eyes. Their movement is quick and herky-jerky, and they are often seen disappearing into walls and corners.

While it may seem like shadow people are a recent phenomenon that only gained traction after paranormal talk show host Art Bell devoted an infamous episode to it on April 12, 2001 (4,500 listeners sent stories in afterward detailing their own shadow men encounters, many with drawings), it actually hails back to ancient times and crosses many cultures. The early Egyptians believed that one of the seven souls of a person was the *khailbut*, a shadow, which was always present, even after death. The Greeks and Romans referred to human souls after death as *shades*. In Greek mythology, if a shade didn't pay the ferryman, Charon, to cross over to the underworld, it would be forced to wander the earth as a ghost. Islamic theology has for centuries talked about preternatural beings known as *djinn*, who, while normally invisible to humans, do sometimes materialize in the form of black smoke.

Across the ocean, the Choctaw American Indian tribe passed down numerous stories about shadow beings, including the *impa shilup*, a great black being that creeps in and devours the souls of individuals who harbor evil or depressing thoughts. Another is the *shilombish*, a person's outside shadow that supposedly remains upon the earth after death until the mourning period is over or family difficulties are resolved. The Cherokee believe shadow people are Indian shamans who have given themselves to the dark side. In modern times, the first literary reference to shadow people occurred in the 1887 short story "Le Horla" by French author Guy de Maupassant. The story tells of a dark presence seen in the periphery of the protagonist's vision and the increasing sense of doom as the presence becomes bolder. In 1953, a Chicago radio station helped popularize the term with its on-air drama "The Shadow People."

While there is a general consensus within the paranormal community affirming the existence of shadow people and their common features, there is a variance of beliefs as to what these beings actually are. Some believe they are ghosts, but because ghosts are usually seen as resembling actual persons or as orbs of light, this explanation is not as popular as others. A more creative theory suggests they are *egregores*, or manifest thought forms, meaning entities created from the negative psychic energy of a particular place and who thrive on the fear and pulsing emotions their presence causes. Some believe they are interdimensional beings and/or time travelers who have found a way to crack the time-space barrier. Others speculate they are extraterrestrials, particularly The Hat Man shadow being, who uses the adornment to cover its unusually-shaped alien head. In a similar vein, paranormal researcher Rosemary Ellen Guiley believes shadow people are djinn, intelligent spirits that inhabit the earth and are able to assume different forms, albeit imperfectly. Guiley explains that according to Arabic lore, the djinn were on earth first and are still angry about being pushed out by humans. Their motives for interacting with humans include curiosity, obsession, playfulness, trickiness, hostility, and malevolence. Guiley also speculates that some shadow people/djinn wear hats and cowls to cover up their imperfectly shaped heads.

One of the more prevalent theories regarding shadow people is that they are, if not outright demons, then ancient evil entities of some sort. Exorcist James Bucknam, who has dealt with many shadow people infestations in his work, cautions people to not engage in behaviors or activities that might attract these entities. Stay away from the occult, crime, substance abuse, and emotional trauma, if possible. And never interact with them if you do see them, he warns. "Shadow people can be one of the most difficult entities to get rid of because they tend to be very tenacious once they decide to visit a person on a regular basis." Bucknam also states that these beings often operate in groups and that their goal "is to bring fear, hopelessness, and pain to that person's life."

The more scientifically minded observers of these shadow phenomena propose physiological and psychological conditions as possible explanations. For example, someone could be experiencing pareidolia, a condition in which the brain incorrectly "sees" familiar images from random patterns of light, shadow, or texture. It is also known that when the left temporoparietal junction in the brain is stimulated, it can create the illusion of a shadow person. Similarly, when our central vision is challenged by low lighting, it is not uncommon to perceive a human figure from what is really just a shadow thrown by, say, a piece of furniture. Then there is the condition of hypnagogia, also known as "waking sleep," a state of semiconsciousness during which a person can at the same time be aware of their environment but also be perceiving images that are being dreamed. People who experience hypnagogia frequently report lights or shadows moving around them, as well as faces and other hallucinations. A feeling of dread often accompanies the visions.

While some shadow people sightings can perhaps be explained scientifically, certainly not all can. What explanation can be given, for example, when two different people see the same apparition? A reader of the online journal *The Line Up* wrote about being awake in bed one night and seeing a shadowy figure come through the bedroom door and make its way to the end of his bed. He could tell by his wife's breathing pattern that she was not asleep and so he asked her if she saw anything. To his surprise, she answered, "You mean that thing standing at the foot of the bed?" Several minutes later, after having just stood there watching the stunned couple, the "thing" faded from their sight.

Further skirting the boundaries of science are the reported instances of people having terrifying physical encounters with these entities. Some have reported being pushed, scratched, or burned. Others have said that shadow people have jumped on their chests and choked them. Then there are the experiences of exorcists and paranormal investigators, who have themselves witnessed the existence of shadow people, often in correlation with hauntings or other such cases of reported paranormal activity.

Whatever they are, whatever their motives for appearing, we will probably never know with any certainty. What we can be fairly certain of is that these shadow creatures live and move among us. They manifest in a variety of manners and circumstances. And they are seen by people of all ages, cultures, and creeds. The following stories are just a sampling of reported encounters with these blacker-than-night beings, but they are more than enough to keep a person watching from the corner of their eye.

The Dining Room Guests

Growing up in Ohio near the edge of Lake Erie, Abby endured extremely harsh, cold winters. It didn't help that her family's house, built during the World War I era, was constantly in need of repairs and impossible to keep properly warm. The warmest room in the house was the kitchen, and that's where Abby did her homework at night. From where she sat at the kitchen table, she had a clear view of the dining room—and the shadow people that frequented it. "I constantly saw shadow people walking around in the dining room," she recounted. "They were normal sized and silent, and though usually out of the corner of my eye, when looked at straight, they would just quietly move on. It wasn't a trick of the eye."

Though she found them distracting, even annoying, she wasn't really frightened by their presence. When she talked to her mother about them, her mother suggested that perhaps they were ghosts and not to worry about them if they weren't hurting anyone. When she turned 18, Abby moved out of the house and only returned for short visits with her parents. On every visit, she still saw the shadow people walking in the dining room. As she thought back to those occasions, she related a sentiment common in other testimonies: "I didn't feel particularly threatened, but I did feel uneasy and not happy they were there. . . . All I can say is the house was creepy."

The Grabber

Mike Ricksecker, in his book *A Walk in the Shadows: A Complete Guide to Shadow People*, related a terrifying incident that happened to him in his childhood. He was about nine years old when something woke him one night from a dead sleep.

He struggled to adjust his sight to the dim lighting of his bedroom, sensing somehow that he was not alone. Slowly a shape came into focus in the corner of his room, a shadowy figure, tall like a man but without specific features. For several minutes, the shadow man stood still and stared at Mike, who at this point was too terrified to move. But then the unthinkable happened. The shadow came over to Mike and reached for him. Mike described the thing's presence as dark and ominous and so black that it blocked out the little bit of light filtering through the window. He tried to scream but could make no sound. Then the shadow grabbed his arms and pulled them up in criss-cross fashion, making Mike feel like he was choking. Suddenly the shadow let go of his arms and abruptly left the room through the open bedroom door. From where he was lying, Mike could see the figure run down the hall, open the linen closet, and disappear inside it. As much as his parents tried to reassure him later that it was only a bad dream, Mike knew otherwise, and that conviction guided his work in later life as a paranormal investigator and historian. As he stated in the introduction to *A Walk in the Shadows*, "I see shadow people. And it's never been a dream."

The Closet Dweller

When Dave was a boy, he and his brothers, his mother, and his uncle all lived in a large house in Edmonton that featured a comfortable lower level where Dave's oldest brother and his uncle had their bedrooms. One night when the boys were home alone, they played hide-and-seek. Dave and his twin were the hiders and their older brother was the seeker. Choosing the best hiding place he could think of, his uncle's closet, Dave shrugged aside his usual uneasiness about the basement and stashed himself behind his uncle's shirts and pants. Soon after sitting down on the floor, Dave felt a hand on his shoulder. Assuming it was his brother, he whispered, "Hiding in here too?" There was no answer, but Dave was focused on being quiet and thought nothing of it. After about five minutes, his body cramped and cold, Dave left the closet and ran upstairs, figuring his brother was behind him. He'll never forget the shock of seeing his twin and older brother sitting on the couch asking where he'd been hiding.

An even greater shock occurred a couple of nights later, though. Dave and his older brother were wrestling in the basement when their WWE theatrics made them tumble into their uncle's room. In the middle of their scuffle, the closet door suddenly swung open on its own. The brothers froze and stared wide-eyed as a tall, dark shadow man walked out of the closet toward them. The boys bolted from the room, Dave crying as he flew into his alarmed mother's arms upstairs. Not long after that, the family moved to a different residence, Dave's mother blaming a rent increase as the reason. Looking back, Dave thinks the move had more to do with his mother finding out a murder had been committed in the house several decades earlier.

Several years later, Dave asked his uncle if he thought his bedroom at the old house was haunted. To his surprise, his uncle answered yes, there had been a presence there. Every few weeks, he told Dave, his closet door would open and a shadow man would come out and stand at the foot of his bed. His uncle didn't believe the shadow man was evil, however, as he felt a rather comforting feeling in its presence and that's why he never complained about it.

The Red-Eyed Hat Man

In her 35 years as a psychic medium, Alyssa had seen her share of spirits. But there was one spectral encounter in particular she will always remember. It happened one night when she woke up around 3:30 a.m. extremely thirsty. She made her way to the kitchen for a cold drink, double-checked (as she always did) that the doors and windows were locked, and started back down the hall to her bedroom. Suddenly she felt goosebumps on her skin and the unmistakable sense of someone watching her. She turned around and saw the reason for her unease. Standing at the end of the hall was a tall black figure wearing what appeared to be a wide-brimmed hat and a long black trench coat. The only discernible features on its face were its glowing red eyes, which were staring right at her. The spirits that visited Alyssa in her work as a medium never caused her concern, as she knew they were the spirits of the departed who were either at peace or looking for peace. This entity before her had a decidedly different impact. She felt fear resonate through her as never before, nearly freezing her in place. But her will to flee proved stronger and she raced back to her bedroom, jumped into bed, and frantically woke her husband to tell him what she saw. Of course, when her husband went out to look, he saw nothing in the hall. Alyssa remains resolute that what she experienced was not a waking dream, even if the image she saw was something from a nightmare.

The Watchers

Mark has seen shadow men his whole life. As a young child, the quick glimpses of shadowy beings didn't affect him too much, but in his teens something changed. The shadows became more solidly black, appeared more frequently, and felt decidedly more evil. He saw them everywhere: his bedroom, at school, in the library, even outside. One day he was out getting wood for the family fireplace when he saw a shadow man walk past him in the dim light of early evening. Several years later, Mark was in his garage when he sensed that something was watching him. He turned and there in the open doorway stood a shadowy man figure. Mark stared in silence at the entity for several moments before running inside the house. When he looked a short time later after calming down, the shadow was gone. Unfortunately, the shadow men haven't stayed gone. Mark has reported that he continues to see them no matter where he is or what he's doing. What disturbs him the most is the "feeling of pure evil" they give off. As anyone would do in his situation, Mark is constantly looking for answers as to what these things are that follow and watch him. And why.

The Laundry Room Lurker

In her book *The Hat Man: The True Story of Evil Encounters*, Heidi Hollis describes a frightening encounter with a shadow man that happened to her sister Keisha. Remembering she had laundry to bring up, Keisha went down to the basement where the washer and dryer were located. She was just about to step off the last step when she looked toward the dryer and saw a tall, dark shadow of a man rise up from behind it. Though she only looked at him for a few seconds before she dropped the laundry basket and ran upstairs screaming, she could clearly recall that he was wearing a rimmed hat and what looked to be a cape. She never went back into the basement alone after that.

The Hospital Creeper

Waverly Hills Sanatorium is known as one of the most haunted places on earth. Located in Louisville, Kentucky, Waverly Hills was a hospital dedicated to treating tuberculosis patients. By the end of its final expansion in 1926, it could house up to 400 patients. Not surprisingly, the hospital was filled with death and suffering on a daily basis, and not just among the afflicted. In 1928, a nurse hanged herself in one of the rooms after finding out she was pregnant by a married doctor with whom she was having an affair. Four years later, another nurse jumped (or was pushed, according to some speculation) off of the roof and plunged several stories to her death. All in all, it is estimated that more than 6,000 people died at the institution. Waverly Hills stopped treating tuberculosis patients in 1961, as the disease had largely been eradicated by then. It reopened a year later as a nursing home until finally closing for good in 1981. The property is now in the care of the Waverly Hills Historical Society, which provides tours to public and private groups, especially those with an interest in the paranormal.

Sightings of shadow people at Waverly Hills during these tours, or during special "ghost hunting" excursions, are not uncommon. Rick Hinton wrote about his overnight ghost-hunting trip in the Indiana *Southside Times*. Among other creepy things he experienced, he wrote: "On the fourth-floor terrace, I was alone and watching a dark shadow following me from within the inner hallway. It was playing hide-and-seek. It would on occasion peek a dark head around the door frames." Paranormal investigator Jay Krow recalled having something invisible brush his arm as it pushed past him. A short time later, after snapping numerous camera shots at shuffling sounds all around him, he finally saw in one shot the distinctive outline of a shadow person. Kansas City paranormal investigator Becky Ray said her experience at Waverly Hills was unlike anything she'd ever seen before: "It's not like one or two, these 'people' are everywhere in this building. . . . They actually move and break the moonlight. I'd never seen anything like it. At one point, they were literally all around us."

Of all the shadow people at Waverly Hills, though, the most infamous is the one known as the Creeper. Unlike other shadow people, the Creeper isn't distinctly human. It manifests as a dark, deformed creature that scurries or shuffles along the floor on all fours. Sometimes it is seen crawling along the ceiling as it slowly approaches unsuspecting visitors. The other thing that sets the Creeper apart from the other shadow beings is the aura of impending doom that accompanies it. Witnesses to the Creeper almost always report being so affected emotionally by it that they have to leave the property to calm down. In the words of one observer, "I never want to feel that again. The dread . . . it was demonic." Some believe that the Creeper may have once been a patient who underwent a medical procedure known as thoracoplasty, a last resort treatment of tuberculosis that involved removing the ribs from the chest wall in order to collapse part of the underlying lung or an abnormal pleural space. An unfortunate side effect, in the unlikely event that the patient survived, was the inability to walk upright due to insufficient bone structure.

The Prankster

Kevin became aware of his psychic abilities at a young age, and it was no surprise, really, as his mother and grandmother were both psychics as well. At age 19, feeling stalled in his metaphysical journey, Kevin began experimenting with a Ouija board in the hopes of reconnecting to the spirit world. It didn't take long. As he recalled, "It took a few tries, but eventually something came through. It scared the hell out of me." That *something* made the hairs on Kevin's neck stand straight up. And then it spelled out on the board: CAN YOU FEEL ME NOW? Several nights later, Kevin woke up in the middle of the night and saw for the first time his new houseguest. A dark shadow in the shape of a tall man wearing a fedora-style hat was pressed against the wall opposite Kevin's bed. Kevin got up to turn on a light but found himself fighting to move forward, as if a strong wind was keeping him from the light switch. After what seemed an eternity, he made it to the light and flipped it on, at which point the shadow man disappeared.

But not for good. The shadow man continued to live in the house even after Kevin moved out, making life interesting but not particularly frightening for Kevin's mother and visiting friends and relatives. As time went on, the entity, who the family had now named "Jack," became more of a prankster than anything. It would open and shut doors, turn lights on and off, and blare the television volume when everyone was sleeping. One night, Kevin and a friend had a tussle with Jack over the television. They would turn it on and Jack would turn it off; it was a struggle that lasted about 20 minutes. Though Kevin could see Jack at the time, his friend could not. Looking back many years later, Kevin speculates that Jack fed off of the attention he was given and grew bolder as a result. Unlike many who encounter shadow people, Kevin never felt a sense of malevolence or menace. In fact, he thinks Jack might have even protected him from a darker entity that followed him home on one occasion. But it could also be, he admits, that Jack was simply protecting his turf.

The Resident Hat Man

As Kathy drove up the long driveway to her friend Mark's house, she started to get an uneasy feeling. It was almost as if someone was watching her. She didn't see anyone, but then again she didn't see much of anything, as Mark's house was out in the country where the only lights were those on the front porches of the generously spaced houses. She parked the car and just happened to look in her rearview window when she saw a pitch-black figure dart around the back of her car. She knew that it was at least as big as a human because it blocked out the light from the garage across the street as it passed. Thinking it was Mark trying to scare her, she looked out all her windows and then, after not seeing anyone, opened her car door. Immediately she felt a rush of energy pushing against her, to the point that she lost her breath. She slammed the door shut and thought about her next move. As she sat there, she began to get that feeling again that something was watching her, only this time it was accompanied by a feeling that "something" was also very near her. That's when she jumped over the gearshift, pushed herself out the passenger side door, and ran to the entrance of the house.

Once inside, Kathy frantically told Mark about her experience in the car. He calmly replied that his property was, in fact, haunted, as it was built over an old cemetery. Oddly, that made Kathy feel a bit better—at least she wasn't losing her mind, she thought. She gladly accepted a glass of wine and sat back as Mark related some spooky episodes other people had experienced in the house, starting with himself.

When he was a boy, Mark said, he would often awake in the middle of the night to find the door that he always shut to be wide open. And standing in the middle of the doorway was a very dark man wearing a brimmed hat. The man never approached him; he just stared at Mark for several moments before fading away. His father also had an unnerving encounter with the mysterious hat-wearing shadow man. Having lived in a house with ghosts for most of his life, Mark's father, Jim, didn't get scared easily. But one incident proved to be a little too much. Jim was on the couch watching television in the middle of the day when he felt something watching him. He looked over his shoulder and there, three feet away, was the Hat Man. Though no facial features were visible, Jim could feel the entity piercing him with his hidden eyes. His voice and body immobilized, all Jim could do was stare back. After about a minute, the Hat Man turned and disappeared down the hallway in the direction of Jim's bedroom. Jim was in no mood to follow it. He set the remote down, grabbed his keys, and left the house for three hours, not returning until the fear inside him had subsided.

Friends of the family were not safe from the Hat Man either. Mark stated that a couple of his girlfriends had the shadow man follow them home after they encountered him at Mark's house. And then there was the incident with his friend Tim, who refused to come around anymore since "that night." Tim had left Mark's house around 10:00 p.m. While driving, he glanced in the rearview mirror and saw, to his horror, the Hat Man sitting behind him. He slammed on his brakes and turned around to get a better look. The seat was empty. Weirdly enough, there was a fallen tree in the road only ten feet from where Tim stopped. Had he not braked after seeing the Hat Man, he likely would have smashed right into it. Was the shadow entity there to thwart disaster? Or was it there to watch the wreck? Tim and Mark couldn't say, but Tim claimed he felt a sense of ill will in the Hat Man's presence. He doubted the shadow being was there to save him.

CHAPTER 3

The Pesky Poltergeist

At one point during the peak of his veterinary practice years, Buster Lloyd-Jones lived with 160 dogs, scores of cats, and innumerable chickens, ducks, goats, ponies, donkeys, and birds, as well as a monkey named Wanda, who felt the need to accompany Buster everywhere perched upon his shoulder. Sharing a homestead with such a menagerie would test the patience of most, but Buster was fond of all his furry and feathered companions, and he saw to all their needs, as best he could, with ingenuity, kindness, and humor. But when an uninvited intruder entered his busy but mostly peaceful domain and began causing all sorts of trouble, Buster's tolerance was tested as never before. It was one thing dealing with flesh and blood animals, varied as they were, but it was another thing entirely dealing with a creature he couldn't even see.

Born into a wealthy English family in 1914, Buster showed an affinity for animals at an early age. When he was four, he fretted at night about bats becoming entangled in the netting surrounding the outside tennis courts. He also worried about the stray cats that wandered onto the estate, especially in bad weather, and would often sneak out to round them up and put them in the empty gardener's cottage until morning. At age five, he declared that he was never going to eat meat again, a vow he kept until his dying day.

The area of West London where the Lloyd-Joneses lived was home to many different species of wildlife, including rabbits, foxes, hedgehogs, and weasels. Young Buster delighted in seeing these animals in their natural habitats, and he was just as excited to learn about the more domestic varieties, such as the goats kept by the local vicar and the cows the town dairyman taught him how to milk. One day, tragedy struck close to home when the family's Irish terrier impaled itself on a jagged railing and was rushed to the vet. From a discreet viewing spot unbeknownst to the adults, Buster watched in awe as the skilled practitioner performed an operation and saved the beloved dog's life. On that very day, Buster announced to his family that he would someday become a veterinarian.

When Buster was an older teen, he answered an ad by a well-known animal society looking for trainees in animal husbandry. His father, who always assumed his son would continue the family clothing business despite all the "nonsense" talk about animals, was outraged and gave Buster an ultimatum: either stay working where he was or leave and never come back. Buster packed his bags and for the next five years trained in animal hospitals all over London, returning home on occasion to see his mother and sisters only when his father was out.

Buster applied for the Royal Veterinary Corps when World War II broke out, but he was medically rejected due to health issues he still suffered as a result of childhood polio. He probably would have stayed in his flat in London, but a surprise visit from his father prompted a change of direction. Appearing contrite and conciliatory, his recently retired father persuaded Buster to move back home where he could open his own practice. The arrangement proved suitable at first, but soon his father became the bitter curmudgeon he had always been and went without speaking to Buster for an entire year before he finally died miserable and unrepentant.

That same year, 1940, proved to be the most harsh and challenging of Buster's career. With food shortages, bombings, and families being torn apart by the war, pets became an extra burden many people either couldn't afford or simply didn't want. As a result, animals by the dozen were brought to Buster to be put down. Though he sympathized with his struggling countrymen, Buster couldn't bring himself to kill perfectly healthy creatures, and so he adopted them, as many as he could, until he ran out of room at his parents' estate and had to move to a larger house. This new residence included ten acres of open land, and here Buster built scads of kennels, catteries, corrals, cages, and coops to house and care for the hundreds of animals now under his charge.

What he didn't arrange for, however, was the sudden unexpected presence of a new tenant that had neither fur nor feathers. In fact, it had no form at all, none that was visible at any rate. But that didn't stop the unseen intruder from making itself known in very tangible and disturbing ways.

Soon after getting settled in the new home with his mother and sisters, Buster was crossing through the garden one day when a rock went whizzing past his head. It landed in the grass a few feet ahead of him, followed by another rock. And then another. Buster twirled around in all directions to see who was throwing the stones at him, but no one was visible. It was possible, he thought, that some neighborhood kids were hiding in the bushes close to the road and throwing from there. But when it happened again the next day, when Buster was in a different part of the yard where there were no bushes to hide behind, the mystery deepened. The stone-throwing continued for days on end with never a culprit in sight. Thankfully, Buster was never directly hit, but several of his windows were, turning the episodes from a puzzle to a problem. Glass was hard to come by in wartime England.

Determined to find out the identity of the jokester, Buster asked the police for help. On three separate occasions, constables camouflaged themselves in greenery, hid in different parts of the grounds, and had Buster walk across a monitored area. And on each occasion, they witnessed stones showering down all around Buster from all different directions. As to where the stones came from or who threw them, the police didn't have a clue. The best they could tell Buster was, "Something very strange is happening here, sir."

The stone-throwing went on intermittently for over a year, but that wasn't the worst of the strange phenomena Buster and his family were subjected to. In the back of the house, leading to what were formerly servants' quarters, was an old dingy stairwell that Buster and members of his staff used quite frequently to get to the clinic area. Until, that is, people were getting strangled on the steps. The first time it happened to Buster, he described it as a pair of hands squeezing his neck, not to the point of choking him but certainly firm enough to get his attention. Though the experience horrified him at the time, Buster's scientific side demanded verification. So he asked other people to go down the stairs, not telling them beforehand what had happened to him, and watched for their reactions. When almost all of them complained of feeling invisible, clammy hands around their necks, Buster closed the stairwell and used an alternate route to the clinic.

At this point, Buster suspected that what he was dealing with was a spirit entity known as a poltergeist, or "noisy ghost," as translated from the German. Unfortunately for Buster and his family, it preferred to be its noisiest around 3:00 a.m., when members of the household were often awakened by the sound of eerie organ music. The mysterious music particularly bothered the multiple dogs that Buster usually had in his room with him at night, and they would cower in a corner in fear, their hackles raised, growling and whining until Buster opened the door to show them no one was outside.

When a group of Army officers, one of them a clergyman, accepted lodging for a few days at Buster's estate, they scoffed at the stories of the phantom organist. That is, until Buster invited them to take turns spending the night in his room. All of them came downstairs the next morning looking tired and ashen-faced. The reverend didn't even last one entire night; he woke Buster out of sleep and demanded his room back, muttering about "that wretched organ."

In addition to middle-of-the-night organ recitals, the ghostly prankster liked to ring doorbells, drop pictures off of walls, sweep objects off of tables, and make any number of strange and unsettling noises. One day after he fell in the garden and twisted his ankle, Buster heard peals of girlish laughter fill the air, but of course no one was anywhere in sight.

The disturbances were serious enough by now that Buster decided to seek the help of a Catholic priest. Having had his injured Airedale successfully treated by Buster on a previous occasion, Father John Riley was more than happy to see what he could do about the vet's "spirit problem." He came over the next day and walked throughout the house, reciting exorcism prayers and sprinkling holy water in each room. For three days after, for the first time in over a year, the disturbances stopped and a peaceful calm descended on the Lloyd-Jones residence. Then, slowly but steadily, the vexations started anew. Rocks rained down, windows broke, the organ played, and chaos once again prevailed.

At his wits' end, Buster recalled that one of the police officers he worked with earlier had suggested he call the Marylebone Spiritualist Association. So he did, and shortly thereafter two women arrived who claimed to be mediums. They listened to Buster's account of the strange happenings that had been going on as they toured the house and grounds, and then told him very matter-of-factly that, yes, he did have a poltergeist. Likely more than one.

With Buster's permission, the women then held a séance in the living room. After a few minutes, one of the women went into a trance and announced that Buster's father was trying to communicate. He was unhappy, she said, and wanted to apologize for his difficult behavior while alive. Buster, of course, was skeptical at first, but when the medium began to describe his father's appearance in detail, as well as facts about his life no one outside the family could have known, he found himself listening in earnest. Especially when his father spoke to him directly through the medium in his unmistakable and well-remembered voice. He begged Buster for forgiveness and said he was a lost soul repentant of his past. As for the poltergeist activity, he was not responsible, he said. He explained that when Buster moved in and converted an outbuilding into kennels, the demolition and construction "disturbed something" that gave rise to the troubling manifestations Buster and his family encountered. He then assured Buster that they would not occur anymore.

From that day on, his father's words held true. The only disturbances at the Lloyd-Jones residence now came from the *natural* world, an unsurprising consequence of living among a multitude of animals. Shortly after his own ghosts had departed, Buster had a conversation with a colleague who had also had a poltergeist experience. This man's specter had thrown a lump of coal at him, hitting him in the eye. In writing his memoirs later in life, Buster reflected on this story, remarking, "So it could have been worse. I might have got a poltergeist with a better aim."

CHAPTER 4

The Bat People

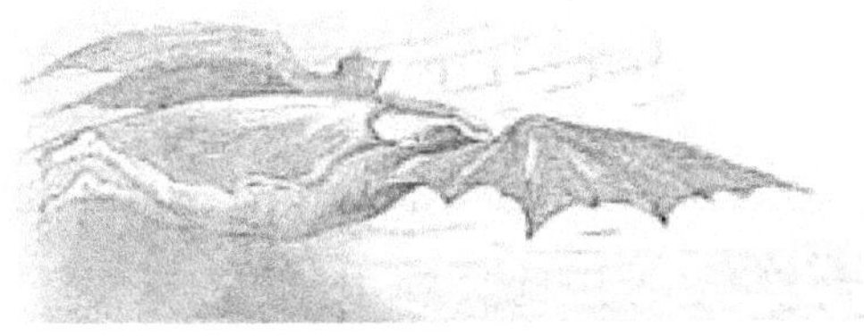

Legends of winged humanoids are present in nearly every culture's oral and written histories. From the Harpies of ancient Greece to the Mothman of modern West Virginia, these fabled figures have dismayed and bedeviled people from all over the globe and from all walks of life. Soldiers, police officers, factory workers, truck drivers, pilots, nurses, housewives, young people, old people—the witness testimonies are as varied as the people themselves. Their one consistency is that they can't explain what they saw.

Among the most fascinating stories are those in which witnesses described the creature they encountered as looking like a bat or at least having bat-like characteristics, most notably black, membranous wings. These stories are also some of the most disturbing, perhaps because of the prevailing imagery of vampires turning into bats, a concept planted into public consciousness by Bram Stoker's novel *Dracula* and further entrenched by countless horror movies ever since. While the following accounts don't involve vampires, per se, they do contain enough troubling details to make a person watch the skies a little more closely and keep the windows closed at night.

Chihuahua, Mexico, 2009

On the evening of March 6, university student Mateo Diaz was driving home from the Universidad Regional del Norte to his home in La Junta when he spotted something large in the middle of the road ahead. The area he was in was fairly isolated, so he approached with caution and made sure his car doors were locked. As he got closer, the object appeared to be a man huddled down under a blanket. Suddenly the figure stood up, took two leaps toward Mateo's car, and unfurled bat-like wings that covered the width of the lane. Terrified, Mateo floored the accelerator and tore down the road at breakneck speed. But, incredibly, the man-bat stayed abreast of the car, flying alongside it while looking in through the passenger's window. Acting out of blind panic, Mateo called his mother, who, from the other end of the line, could hear the roar of the racing car and asked what was going on. His voice broken by sobs, Mateo tried to describe the monster chasing him, but soon gave in to despair and simply wailed, "I'm going to die! I'm going to die!" After about fifteen minutes, Mateo came to a more heavily trafficked area, prompting the creature to veer away from the car and fly off into the dark.

Finally arriving home, the young man collapsed in his mother's arms. "I had never heard him like that, and much less seen him in the state he arrived," she recalled. "He was shivering, pale, and in the midst of a nervous breakdown." When questioned later, Mateo insisted that what he saw was no illusion. He described his pursuer as tall and dark, with bloodshot eyes and two pairs of wings, one large, the other small. The creature also had small "kangaroo-like" hands that it used to repeatedly strike the passenger side window. Its face, while human-looking, was covered in some sort of dark fur. As Mateo and his family had outstanding reputations in the community, city and university officials found no reason to denounce his story, which was carried in the newspaper *El Heraldo de Chihuahua*. For weeks afterward, numerous people reported seeing the man-bat in the same general region, including a farmhand who claimed to see the creature struggling in some netting used to shield young plants from hail. Days later, sheep at several nearby ranches were found with their throats slit and their tails cut.

Holmen, Wisconsin, 2006

Driving home late one night from La Crosse, Wisconsin, to their home in Holmen, a man by the name of Wohali and his 25-year-old son had just rounded a hill near a wooded area on Briggs Road when they were suddenly dive-bombed by a creature that defied belief. Standing before them on the hood of their car was a six-foot tall brownish-gray being with large leathery wings that spanned half the width of the road. The thing had man-like legs with clawed talons and piercing yellow eyes set within a diabolical face that reminded Wohali of a horror movie vampire. The creature tried smashing their windshield with its feet, but then, for whatever reason, suddenly veered off and shot straight up toward the treetops at lightning speed. "I've never seen anything move like that," Wohali later stated.

As it flew off, the fiend delivered a spine-tingling shriek that affected the men in such a visceral manner that they became violently sick and had to pull over. The high-pitched sound stayed in their heads days after the attack and continued to make them feel unwell. Wohali also reported that strange noises and an eerie vibe plagued his house for some time afterward, causing his dog to hide under the bed. He wondered if the creature they encountered was some sort of supernatural entity that had "projected" negative energies onto them. It seemed too big a coincidence to dismiss.

Houston, Texas, 1953

Houston, Texas, in the summer can be unbearable, especially in the days before air conditioning was standard in all homes. Trying to beat the heat was exactly why Hilda Walker and her neighbors Judy Meyer and Howard Philips were sitting out on their front porches in the middle of the night on June 18, 1953. Had they not, they wouldn't have witnessed one of the most extraordinary sightings ever of a flying humanoid. At approximately 2:30 a.m., Hilda noticed a large shadow moving across the lawn about twenty-five feet away. At first she thought it was a reflection of a big moth from a nearby streetlight. But then the shadow bounced up into a pecan tree. The three neighbors looked up at the tree—and couldn't believe what they saw. A man-like figure about six-and-a-half feet tall with bat wings attached to his back hovered near the top of the tree. He was clearly visible, as he was awash with a glowing yellow light that mesmerized the stunned onlookers for a good thirty seconds or more. Then the light began to fade and the figure vanished. Finally finding her voice, Judy let out a scream. In an interview later, Hilda recalled, "Immediately afterward we heard a loud swoosh over the housetops across the street. It was like a white flash of a torpedo-shaped object." Howard made a similar claim: "We looked across the street and saw a flash of light rise from another tree and take off like a jet." The next morning, Hilda filed a police report of the shocking encounter. "I may be nuts, but I saw it, whatever it was . . . I sat there stupefied. I was amazed."

Chesterland, Ohio, 2016

James had always considered himself a skeptic about things like ghosts, aliens, Bigfoot, and other such "unexplained" phenomena. That is, until one summer night in Ohio when he experienced something for himself that he had no explanation for. He was driving a Freightliner box truck west on Rt. 322 toward Chesterland, happy that the moon was helping to light the way through the rural hills. At around 3:45 a.m., he saw a large dark figure suddenly come out of nowhere right at him. He slammed on the brakes and instinctively ducked down, expecting a face-on collision at windshield level. Sure enough, James heard a loud thud as the thing hit the front of the truck, rolled over the top, and hit the flat aluminum box behind the cab. He pulled over as soon as he could, about 75 yards from the impact, jumped out and inspected the box, looking for any trace of whatever it was he had hit. Other than a depression in the aluminum, nothing else was visible.

He went around to the rear of the truck and that's when he saw it, a dark mass lying in the middle of the road, quiet, still . . . lifeless. Or so he thought. As James stared, the figure suddenly rose up on two legs and stared right back at him.

James's blood ran cold. Illuminated by the moonlight, the creature before him was clearly not human, even though it stood like a man at about six feet tall. Men didn't have wings, and this thing did, huge bat-like wings; and men didn't have orange/red eyes, which the creature in front of him used to transfix James in a state of frozen terror. Just as James thought he was about to pass out, the thing spread its wings, leaped up and flew off. Still dumbfounded but eager to get away before *it* came back, James hurriedly climbed into his truck and raced off to Chesterland. He later told paranormal researcher and author Lon Strickler, "The thing that stood out the most to me were its eyes. I'll never forget how much they mesmerized me with that fiery orange color. It was almost like it could see into my soul. It only lasted for a couple of seconds, but I did feel some sort of connection with it. I was very much afraid of it, though."

Mount Rainier Foothills, Washington, 1994

Better known for its sightings of the large, hairy, two-legged beast commonly known as Bigfoot or Sasquatch, the Pacific Northwest has also had its fair share of other reported cryptid creatures, including one from 1994 that combines the best of Bigfoot and Batman. Dubbed "Batsquatch" by locals after word got out about the sighting, it remains a singularly unique entry in Washington State cryptid lore.

On April 23, at about 9:30 p.m., 18-year-old Brian Canfield was driving home to the isolated settlement known as Camp One near the foothills of Mount Rainier when suddenly his truck's engine shut down and he came to a stop in the middle of the road. As he sat there wondering what was wrong, a large figure slowly descended into the beam of his headlights about thirty feet in front of him. Brian had never seen anything like it. Nine feet tall and stout, the creature slowly gravitated down on two clawed feet. A pair of wings were folded behind its broad shoulders. It had blue-tinted fur, tufted ears, yellowish eyes, and a wolf-like face but with straight teeth instead of fangs. It landed with a dust-raising thud. And then it fixed its gaze on Brian. "It was standing there staring at me, like it was resting, like it didn't know what to think," Brian told journalist C.R. Roberts of the *Tacoma News Tribune*. "I was scared. It raised the hair on me." The creature continued to stare at Brian for several minutes until it finally unfolded its wings, rose up, and slowly flew off toward the mountains. The turbulence from the creature flapping its wings in takeoff caused Brian's truck to sway.

After the beast was gone from sight, the truck inexplicably started up on its own. Brian raced home and woke his parents. "His mouth was dry, he was pale, his hair was standing on end," recalled his mother. Brian convinced his father and a neighbor to go back with him to the sight of the encounter. Armed with a gun and a camera, the three men returned to that section of road but found no trace of the creature or anything else unusual.

After interviewing Brian and talking to his family and friends, journalist Roberts became convinced of his credibility. "I believe his story," he wrote in his column afterward. "I believe he saw something that night a week ago. I have no idea what he saw. But I believe Brian Canfield."

Monterrey, Mexico, 2004

In the early morning hours of January 16, 2004, police officer Leonardo Samaniego Gallegos was on his rounds in an eastern suburb of Monterrey, Mexico, when he suddenly saw something big and black fall from a tree a short distance in front of his patrol car. Only the figure didn't fall all the way to the ground; it hovered above it. Samaniego turned his high beams on and saw a tall humanoid with brownish skin covered in what appeared to be black clothing or fur. As the light hit its face, it covered its eyes and then, according to Samaniego, it became angry. It sped toward him, grabbed the patrol car, and shook it violently. Startled and fearful, the officer spun the car around in circles in an attempt to shake off his attacker while at the same time calling for backup on his radio. The creature then started smashing the windshield, prompting Samaniego to shift into reverse and then gun the car forward. Unfortunately, he lost control, crashed the vehicle, and was knocked unconscious. Fortunately, Samaniego wasn't seriously injured and was quickly revived by paramedics who arrived at the scene minutes later. By then, there was no sign of the officer's mysterious assailant. Following protocol, Samaniego was taken to the hospital and subjected to a series of psychological and toxicology tests, all of which came back normal.

News of Officer Samaniego's encounter initiated a flurry of reports of similar sightings in the region. One resident of Monterrey, who was a member of the UFO Club of Nuevo Leon, came forward with a video purportedly showing a human-looking figure flying over the hills outside the city. Soon other residents claimed to see this same figure, which would come to be known as "La Bruja de Guadalupe" or "The

Witch of Guadalupe." Interestingly, about two weeks before Officer Samaniego's attack, another police officer in the same department, Manuel Sifuentes, reported a strange incident that happened to him. He was leaving the police station on foot when suddenly a black creature with a large stick swooped down out of the sky toward him. As it passed close, Sifuentes recalled, "I felt much cold as if I had gotten into a freezer full of ice." When questioned later, he claimed he was certain that the entity was a witch and that he could feel the "bruja's" energy go right through him.

In most of the accounts of "bat people" or other winged humanoids, the creatures are described as male. But not always. In the following stories, the flying figures are distinctly female, with decidedly female features and allures.

Da Nang, Vietnam, 1969

On a sultry summer night in August 1969, Private Earl Morrison and two of his buddies from the U.S. 1st Marine Division were on guard duty outside the city of Da Nang, Vietnam. Sitting atop a bunker, they were thankful for the moon's illumination and the stillness of the evening air as they kept a sharp lookout for Vietcong. But it wouldn't be the Vietnamese enemy the men encountered later that night. Rather, it was something so unexpected and so unexplainable that it would take three years before Earl Morrison was ready to talk publicly about it. When he was finally persuaded to by UFO researcher Don Worley, he swore that what he was about to describe well exceeded the capacity of his imagination.

Their sentry duty thus far had been uneventful for the first part of the evening, according to Morrison. But then at around 1:30 a.m., something made all three men look up into the sky. "We saw this figure coming toward us. It had a kind of glow and we couldn't make out for sure what it was at first. It started coming toward us real slowly. And all of a sudden we saw what looked like wings, like a bat only it was gigantic compared to what a regular bat would be. After it got close enough so we could see what it was, it looked like a woman. A naked woman. She was black, everything was black. Her skin was black, her body was black, the wings were black, everything was black. But it glowed. It glowed in the night— kind of a greenish cast to it."

The winged woman hovered over the men for several minutes, so close to them at one point that "she blotted out the moon." Describing the creature's wings, Morrison said that they had arms attached to them, each with a hand and fingers, and were covered with membrane from the wings. When she flapped them, "it looked like her arms didn't have any bones in them because they were limber just like a bat." The creature had gotten as near as seven feet above the men's heads before she veered back off into the sky. The awestruck Marines watched her for several more minutes as she flew slowly and gracefully out of their sight.

The men immediately reported what they had seen to their superiors, but were received with abject skepticism. Neighboring posts were asked if anything out of the ordinary had been spotted that night, but all replies came back negative. When asked during his interview why they didn't panic or shoot at the creature, Morrison answered, "We couldn't do anything. We didn't know what to do. We just froze. We just watched what was going over 'cause we couldn't believe our eyes."

While the sighting in Vietnam by Morrison and his comrades was incredible, none of the men described it as frightening or horrific. Perhaps the fact that the men displayed weapons was enough to keep the creature from exhibiting any aggression. Or perhaps it was simply non-confrontational by nature. Interestingly, many years later, an acquaintance of Morrison's also reported seeing a "bat woman," this one, however, far removed from Southeast Asia, and bearing a decidedly different vibe.

Albuquerque, New Mexico, 1980s

Martin Garcia had had an uneventful night of eating a pizza in front of the television before finally heading off to bed. He had stayed up later than usual, his routine a bit off because his wife was away visiting her mother in Texas and he was not used to going to bed without her. Once he got settled and was close to nodding off, he heard a tapping on the window. In his muddled state, he assumed it was a bird tapping its beak against the glass. But then he thought, what bird is out at night? It had to be a bat, he remembered thinking. A bat that had flown into the window accidentally. Then he heard a woman's voice, and he came fully awake instantly. "I swear that I heard a voice outside of the second-floor bedroom window," he recalled. Martin walked over to investigate and rubbed his eyes in disbelief. Floating in front of him at eye level was a dark female figure. Though her features were shadowed, in the light of the moon he could clearly see that she was smiling at him. And then she asked him to open the window.

Martin jumped back in shock and fear. He remembered hearing the story of the glowing winged woman his buddy at work saw while stationed in Vietnam. Although his friend wasn't hurt by that creature, Martin didn't want to take any chances with this one. In his written testimony, he noted that there were several differences between the "bat woman" his buddy saw and the figure outside his window, the first being that this woman wasn't naked. "She wore some kind of dark, swirling nightgown-type garment. It kind of reminded me of pictures of old burial shrouds." The other significant difference was that Martin's visitor had no wings, at least as far as he could see. "She seemed to just bob up and down outside the window."

As if the vision before him wasn't strange enough, the ethereal woman then started singing. But it wasn't like any song Martin had heard before. In fact, he can't remember any words, only a hypnotic melody that wormed its way into his head and almost lulled him into opening the window wide. Just as he started to, a warning voice sounded in his head and he slammed the window shut, remembering all the horror movies he had seen in which the characters were told that evil entities, like vampires, had to be invited in. Martin didn't know if the creature outside was a vampire, but he sure wasn't going to let it in now that his mind was clear. He ran over to the wall, took down a large crucifix, and held it up in front of the window. The woman laughed. As Martin continued to hold up the crucifix, the laugh turned into more of a mocking cackle, a horrid sound that sent shivers up Martin's spine. Finally, the woman turned away and flew off into the darkness, flapping what did appear then to be wings.

When Martin's wife returned home after a few days, he told her of his encounter with the flying woman. She listened attentively, without question or ridicule, and then told him that the very night it happened, she had dreamed that he was being threatened by something evil. She awoke in a panic, immediately knelt by the side of her bed, and prayed for his protection. Martin believes his wife's timely diligence paid off. He was never visited by the "bat woman" again.

CHAPTER 5

The Butcher of Oz

Those fortunate enough to only briefly cross paths with the ruddy-cheeked, bespectacled blonde would most likely remember a pleasant but unremarkable woman. Those who knew her a little better, co-workers and neighbors, would have described her as a hard worker who liked to socialize at the local watering hole. Those who knew her more intimately, however, would know that it was best not to make her angry. And if, God forbid, you did make her angry on one of her "bad days," the best thing you could do would be to run. Unfortunately, 46-year-old John Price couldn't run fast enough or far enough, though the blood trail discovered by police at the scene of his murder showed that he desperately tried. The other discoveries by police that day were of such horrifying and unprecedented caliber that they made headlines around the world. The small town of Aberdeen, Australia, was suddenly in the spotlight, its people in shock and disbelief over the gruesome news that broke on March 1, 2000. Story after story described one of the grisliest crime scenes in Australian history. John Price wasn't just stabbed. He was butchered, skinned, dismembered, cooked, and eaten. His murderer, still on the scene and covered in his blood when police arrived, was a woman who felt scorned because "Pricey" refused to marry her. Katherine Mary Knight, without question, had had a very, very bad day.

Some would say that Katherine was doomed from the start. She and her twin sister were born in 1955 after her mother, Barbara, left her husband, Jack, for her husband's co-worker, Ken Knight. Ken was a vicious alcoholic who beat and raped Barbara daily. She accepted the abuse and even talked openly to her daughters about intimate details of her sex life. When Katherine became sexually active in her teenage years and complained about her lovers wanting to do things she didn't like, Barbara bluntly told her to "put up with it and stop complaining." Men were brutal and disgusting by nature, she repeatedly told Katherine, and they were incapable of being kind or faithful. If nothing else was impressed upon Katherine by her mother, these words certainly were.

In school, Katherine was mostly regarded as a congenial student, but only until someone or something upset her. Then she would fly into uncontrollable and frightening rages, one of which left her injured when a teacher had no choice but to fight back in self-defense against Katherine's knife-wielding attack. Contrarily, when she wasn't throwing violent fits or bullying smaller children, Katherine was often a model student and even won awards for her good behavior.

Katherine's erratic school years came to an end at age 15 when she quit school for good and entered the workforce. Barely able to read or write, her choices were somewhat limited, but a year after dropping out she obtained what she described as her "dream job," cutting up offal (the internal organs of food animals) and cleaning up the waste at the Aberdeen Abattoir. She displayed such enthusiasm and proficiency at her job that she was quickly promoted to de-boning the livestock and was given her own set of professional abattoir knives. So proud was she of these blades that she took them home every night to clean and sharpen. Then she hung them over her bed so they "would always be handy if I needed them," a practice she continued for years and at every place she lived.

In 1974, Katherine married David Kellett, a hard-drinking truck driver she met at work. Setting a rather ominous tone for the marriage, Katherine's mother took the slightly intoxicated David aside before the wedding ceremony and told him, "You better watch this one or she'll f--king kill you. . . . She's got a screw loose somewhere." David learned the hard truth to those words that very night when he woke to find Katherine strangling him in bed. He managed to push her away and asked her what she was doing. Katherine angrily declared that she wasn't yet satisfied after three rounds of intercourse and how dare he fall asleep.

From that point on, the marriage was marked by near-daily outbursts of Katherine's anger. One night not long into the marriage, David awoke again to find Katherine hovering over him, this time with one of her abattoir knives at his neck. She demanded to know if it was true that truck drivers have women in every town. After somehow convincing her that he wasn't seeing anyone on the side, Katherine hung the knife back over their bed.

In early 1976, heavily pregnant with their first child, Katherine flew into another rage when David came home late from a darts competition. As he stumbled in through the door past midnight, Katherine flew at him and smashed him in the back of the head with a frying pan. Right before that, she had burned all his clothes and shoes in the backyard. David fled to a neighbor's house, where he collapsed into unconsciousness. Scans taken at the hospital showed he had a fractured skull, but despite urging by police, David decided not to press charges when Katherine appeared at his bedside remorseful and distraught.

The physical violence and emotional stress from living with Katherine soon proved too much for David, however, and in May 1976, shortly after the birth of their daughter, Melissa Ann, he left Katherine for another woman and moved to Queensland. Katherine did not react well. She was seen the very next day pushing Melissa's stroller down a busy street, shaking it violently from side to side as the baby wailed from within. Concerned citizens intervened and Katherine was admitted to St. Elmo's Hospital, where she was diagnosed with postnatal depression.

After spending several weeks in the hospital, Katherine was reunited with her daughter, but apparently her "recovery" wasn't quite complete. On her next stroller outing with baby Melissa, Katherine wheeled the infant onto nearby train tracks and left her there shortly before the next train was due to arrive. Luckily, a local man who was foraging near the railway line discovered the abandoned child and rescued her before tragedy struck. In the meantime, Katherine was keeping busy in town by threatening to kill people with a stolen axe. Once again, after the police intervened, Katherine was taken to St. Elmo's. Due to either an egregious oversight or criminal endangerment on the part of the staff, Katherine was deemed mentally fit within 24 hours and was allowed to sign herself out the following day.

Soon after returning home, Katherine set her sights on exacting revenge against David. Using one of her abattoir knives, she slashed the face of a female co-worker and forced the terrified woman to drive her to Queensland. At a midpoint along the way, they stopped at a service station, where Katherine's hostage was able to escape and call for help. When the police arrived, they found Katherine with a new hostage, a young mechanic who thought for sure his neck was about to be slashed by the crazy woman holding a knife to it. Thankfully, the young man's neck was left intact when officers finally disarmed Katherine and tackled her to the ground. She was placed in the Morisset Psychiatric Hospital where she candidly told nurses she had every intention of killing not only David and his girlfriend but also the mechanic who serviced David's car and thereby helped him to leave her. When police told David of Katherine's recent activities and her intended murder plans, he reacted in a way no one could have guessed. Feeling guilty for his wife's psychological breakdown and determined to set things right, he left his girlfriend and moved back to Aberdeen with his mother to take care of Katherine.

On August 9, 1976, Katherine was released into the care of her husband and mother-in-law. Looking to get a fresh start, the reunited family moved to a suburb of Brisbane, where Katherine obtained a new job at the local abattoir, Dinmore Meatworks. In March 1980, Katherine gave birth to the couple's second daughter, Natasha Maree. Despite the seeming stability of their home life, the day-to-day reality was anything but. Katherine continued her violent outbursts and dark periods of depression even while receiving medication and therapy. Though no one would have blamed David if he left again, this time it was Katherine who ended the relationship. In 1984, in typical Katherine fashion, she left without warning, moving herself and her daughters back to Aberdeen and leaving David with a house stripped of its contents. She returned to her job at the Aberdeen abattoir but injured her back a year later, forcing her onto a disability pension.

In 1986, Katherine met 38-year-old David Saunders, a miner from the nearby town of Scone. After becoming an official couple, Saunders moved in with Katherine but kept his old apartment, which proved to be a wise decision for those frequent occasions when Katherine accused him of cheating and threw him out. After one particularly nasty argument, Katherine grabbed Saunder's 8-week-old dingo puppy and slashed its throat in front of her shocked partner, declaring that's what would happen to him if she ever caught him having an affair. Amazingly, the relationship continued and produced a daughter, Sarah, in 1988. Prompted by the birth of his child, Saunders put a deposit down on a house, which the couple eventually paid for when Katherine's worker's compensation package came through. In a nod to her unconventional tastes, Katherine set to work decorating the new abode in slaughterhouse chic, covering every foot of space with animal skins, horns, skulls, rusted animal traps, machetes, rakes, pitchforks, leather jackets, and old boots.

However, a new house and baby weren't enough to keep the relationship going. After coming home from a night of drinking, Saunders was met at the door by an enraged Katherine, who hit him in the face with an iron and then stabbed him in the stomach with a pair of scissors. Saunders escaped back to his apartment in Scone but then quickly decided it was best to go into hiding completely. When he returned several months later to see his daughter, he was stunned to discover that Katherine had gone to the police and managed to obtain an Apprehended Violence Order against him, effectively keeping him away from her and Sarah.

In May 1990, Katherine began what would be the shortest but most stable relationship she had ever had, this time with a man named John Chillingworth, a recovering alcoholic who had worked with Katherine at the abattoir. In an interview years later, Chillingworth admitted he knew Katherine had a bad side but he never felt threatened by her. They had one violent episode that he could recall, an argument that culminated in Katherine smacking his glasses off his face and breaking his false teeth, and he in turn slapping her in the face. Nonetheless, the couple had a son, Eric, in 1991, and stayed together for another two years. Chillingworth broke off the relationship after discovering Katherine was having an affair with the man who would become her last lover and ultimate victim, John Price.

John Charles Price, known to his friends as "Pricey," was well-liked by everyone who knew him, including his ex-wife with whom he shared three children. In 1995, Katherine left her bizarrely decorated home and moved into Price's considerably less shoddy bungalow. By all accounts, Katherine and John and their respective children got along fairly well for the first couple of years together. John made a good salary, so money was never an issue, and aside from a few vociferous arguments, the relationship appeared solid. But there was one thing that nagged at Katherine: Price's refusal to marry her.

In 1998, this point of contention came to a head after a heated argument in which Price once again said no to the idea of marriage. In retaliation, Katherine videotaped some items Price had procured from work and had stashed in a cupboard at his house. She then presented the videotape to Price's employers, who subsequently fired Price for stealing. Price argued that the items in question, out-of-date medical kits, had been marked for the trash bin, but his pleas failed to sway his bosses' decision. Furious over losing his job of 17 years, Price kicked Katherine out of his house. A few months later, the two began seeing each other again, but Price still refused to have Katherine live with him.

Price found a new job at Bowditch and Partners Earth Moving and within a year was made supervisor. While that part of his life was going well, his relationship with Katherine was steadily getting worse. Fights between them became more commonplace as well as more violent. On February 21, 2000, he was forced to flee his house after Katherine stabbed him in the chest with a knife. That was the last straw, as far as Price was concerned. Fearing for the safety of himself and his children, Price obtained a restraining order against Katherine eight days later. That same afternoon, Price told his co-workers that if he didn't come to work the next day, it was because Katherine had killed him. His co-workers tried to convince him not to go home that night, but Price said if he didn't, Katherine might kill his kids.

Price arrived home that evening to find that Katherine had sent his children to a friend's house for a sleepover. She herself was not at the house. Wisely, Price spent the evening at his neighbor's, but then not-so-wisely returned home around 11:00 to go to bed. Katherine, meanwhile, had been spending the early evening hours videotaping herself with her children and granddaughter, singing nursery rhymes to them and making odd comments about hoping to see them again after this "special" time together. Afterward, Katherine took her family to a Chinese restaurant, another out-of-the-ordinary act that prompted Natasha to offhandedly remark to her mother, "I hope you're not going to kill Pricey and yourself."

Later that night, Katherine returned to Price's house. While Price was sleeping, she watched TV for a short while, then got up and took a shower. Clean and attired in a new negligee she had bought earlier that day, she then woke Price and had sex with him. According to a statement she gave later to authorities, Price fell asleep afterward and "that's it," as she went on to claim she could remember nothing from that point on. But Katherine's claim of "that's it" would prove to be a far cry from the very busy timeline police ultimately pieced together after discovering the hellish scene at John Price's house the next morning.

When Price didn't arrive at work the next day, his employer sent a worker to check on him. The worker was met by a neighbor, who was also concerned when he noticed Price's car still in the driveway. The two men banged on Price's bedroom window in an attempt to wake him, but when they noticed blood on the front door, they called the police. Officers Furlonger and Matthews were the first to arrive on the scene. After being filled in about Price's unstable girlfriend and seeing for themselves the blood on the door, the officers went around the house and kicked in the back door. As they made their way down the dimly lit hallway, they encountered a sheet of some sort hanging from the ceiling. Pushing it aside, Officer Matthews was surprised to find it was cold and wet to the touch. He was also surprised that suddenly his left arm was bleeding. Only it wasn't his arm that was bleeding, as his brain quickly surmised. It was the "sheet" he had just touched. Inspecting it more closely, the officers were horrified to see that what was hanging from a hook in the archway was actually the skin of John Price, expertly removed to form a non-broken hide complete with eye holes and still slick with blood.

Further entering the house, they found an even more gruesome discovery. "I saw a torso on the ground without a head, without any genitalia," recounted Officer Matthews. The skinned and dismembered body of John Price lay in a pool of blood on the lounge floor. Price had been stabbed 37 times in both his front and back, with many of the slashes puncturing vital organs and severing the aorta. The body had then been butchered and skinned by a highly skilled hand using an extremely sharp instrument. By someone who knew how to remove the entirety of the skin from the top of the head to the feet. Police found their flayer in short order in the nearby bedroom. Alive but unresponsive, it was quickly determined that Katherine had taken a cocktail of pills in a suicide attempt.

While an ambulance was being called for Katherine, police continued to find grisly components of the crime scene. The kitchen held the worst sight: a large soup pot containing the skinned head of John Price bobbing around in a mixture of potatoes and cabbage. Other parts of Price had been neatly served up on plates in the dining room, where a table had been set with place cards indicating where John's children were to sit. Police found a third meal plate in the backyard, where they speculated Katherine threw it after eating some of it herself. By now, more police had been called to the scene, with several refusing to enter the house, stating it was too much for them to handle. The lead detective on the case, Bob Wells, described it as the worst he had seen in 20 years on the job. A fingerprint technician resigned the next day after working on the site.

Interviews with Katherine after she recovered proved to be futile. She held firm to her story that after having sex with Price, she blacked out for the rest of the night and remembered nothing. Investigators were nonetheless able to piece together exactly what had happened from the overwhelming amount of forensic evidence. According to expert court testimony, Price was stabbed with a butcher's knife while he was sleeping. Blood evidence showed that he awoke and tried to turn on the light before running through the house in an effort to escape. He made it through the front door but either fell or was dragged back into the hallway where he bled to death. Shortly afterward, Katherine was recorded at an ATM, where she withdrew $1,000 from Price's bank account. Then, over the course of the next several hours, she proceeded to dismember, skin, and cook various body parts of her ex-lover.

Katherine's initial offer to plead guilty to manslaughter on the grounds of diminished responsibility was promptly rejected by Justice Barry O'Keefe, who noted that the precise methodology used to remove John Price's skin could not have been done by a person acting irrationally or crazed. A trial date was set for October 2001. However, the day before the trial was to begin, Katherine unexpectedly changed her plea to guilty. An overnight mental examination to see if Katherine truly understood the nature and consequences of her plea determined that she was indeed sane enough for the court's satisfaction. On November 8, 2001, Justice O'Keefe sentenced Katherine to life imprisonment and ordered her papers to be marked "never to be released." It was the first time in Australian history a woman had ever been sentenced to life without parole.

Katherine is living out her years in Silverwater Women's Correctional Center, where she spends her time knitting, painting, and taking pottery classes. The other inmates call her "Nanna." Though not confirmed, it is reasonable to believe that she is not permitted to work in the kitchen.

CHAPTER 6

The Naughty Doll

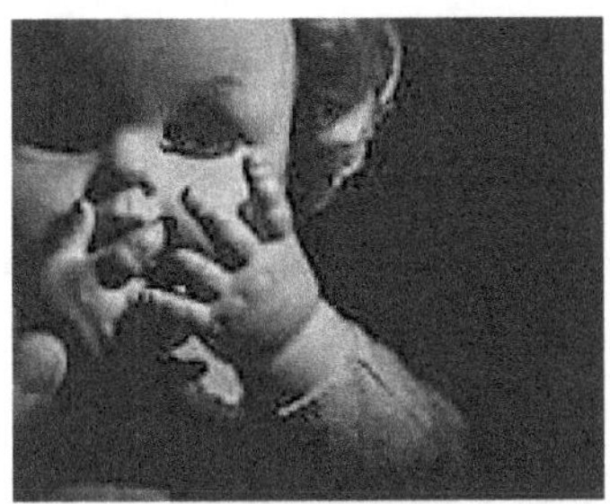

Paul Kramer was a healthy, happy ex-Marine who worked for a rental property company during the week and visited antique shops and yard sales with his wife, Terry, on the weekends. And if anyone gave him a hard time about his leisure activities, they were apt to get Paul's drill sergeant alter ego in their face. Not much unnerved the Vietnam vet, but in the spring of 1989, a series of peculiar and unexplainable events rattled his worldview unlike anything he had ever encountered. They all centered around what Paul would only refer to as "the doll."

Paul and Terry had spent a beautiful April morning scouring the numerous antique shops along the western bank of the Susquehanna River in Harford County, Maryland. About to call it quits and grab some lunch, they entered one last shop and were immediately drawn to a large, exquisitely dressed doll that had been positioned on a small table all by itself. The doll's short brown hair with frosted tips, along with its soft plastic features, gave it a modern, Barbie-like style. But what truly set the doll apart from its more common antique shop porcelain cousins was the elegant white wedding-like gown adorning it. Obviously handmade from silk and lace, the dress itself would command a large price, thought the Kramers. Expecting to hear that the doll was at least $100, Paul and Terry couldn't believe it when the shop owner told them it was only $10. That was a bargain they simply couldn't pass up.

As soon as they got home, Terry set the doll on top of the television console. The doll's feet had been nailed to a block of wood wrapped in the same material as its dress, so standing it up was no problem. It made for a captivating centerpiece in the living room. The Kramer's 14-year-old daughter, Ellen, however, had reservations. A few days after bringing the doll home, Ellen told her parents that the doll's eyes followed her whenever she passed through the living room. Chalking it up to teenage imagination, Paul did privately agree that the doll's dark blue eyes, shrouded in smoky eyeshadow and long black lashes, could create the illusion of watchfulness. Nevertheless, he soon forgot about his daughter's claims.

A few weeks later, Ellen had a new concern: in the afternoons when only she and her brother, Mark, were home, she heard the sound of someone roller skating in the hallway. Mark later told his parents that he heard it too. Mark also claimed to have seen doorknobs in the house turning by themselves. Up to this point, neither Paul nor Terry had seen or heard anything unusual, but that was about to change.

Terry bought some new home decor items and decided to put something different on top of the television. She moved the doll to their bed, but because it kept falling over, she asked

Paul to take the wooden block off the doll's feet. Paul later recalled that for some strange reason, he didn't feel right about taking the block off, but it did help to keep the doll sitting upright. For the next several days, nothing out of the ordinary occurred, but then one night as Paul was passing by the bedroom, he noticed that the doorknob on the closed door was turning. He didn't think anyone was in there, but he waited to see if someone did indeed come out. When no one did, he opened the door and walked in. The room was empty. The only figure in it was the doll, sitting where she had been placed earlier, in the center of the bed.

While that little oddity had him shaking his head, the next "encounter" had him shaking from head to toe. It was a Saturday night and Terry's mother had come over for dinner with the family. It started getting late, and as it looked like the two women were going to continue talking for a while over wine, Paul said his goodnights and headed to the bedroom. Turning down the bed, he moved the doll to a chair in the corner of the room, as he and Terry did every night. Paul was tired and he expected to fall asleep fast, but within a minute of his head hitting the pillow, he heard a rustling sound that roused him from his drowsiness. He sat up and looked toward the noise. There in the corner sat a little girl about five years old. She had short blonde hair parted down the middle, and though there was an unearthly glow about her, she looked incredibly real to Paul, "fleshy," as he later described her. She was holding the doll.

Paul jumped out of bed, grabbed his clothes, and dressed on the run down the hallway. Rushing into the kitchen, he yelled out, "There's a little girl in the bedroom!" Of course, when Paul and the women went to investigate, there was no one in the room. Only the doll was visible, perched in the corner where Paul had placed her. Terry and her mother thought Paul had had a "waking nightmare" and offered him a glass of wine to calm his nerves. Later, when Paul went back to bed, he turned on all the lights.

Enough strange things had happened to the family by now to prompt Paul and Terry to consider that they had a paranormal problem. They began a systematic examination of all the objects they recently brought into the house to try to determine if one of them could be the cause of the eerie activity. But for some unexplainable reason, neither of them thought about the most obvious source: the doll. When asked about this by an interviewer a few years later, Paul simply replied, "I don't know."

The Kramers' purge of all possible cursed knickknacks and other assorted sundries did have one positive side effect: it lightened the load when they moved to a new house in a new neighborhood. The family happily settled into their new abode, relishing the larger space and updated fixtures. Even their dog, Max, seemed happier in it. For the first few weeks, Max claimed the space under Paul and Terry's bed as his sleeping spot. But when Terry finally finished unpacking and put the doll back on their bed, Max suddenly wouldn't enter the bedroom anymore. Equally disturbing, Ellen and Mark reported hearing roller skates in the house again.

As if a fog was lifting from their minds, Paul and Terry slowly came to the realization that the doll was the source of their problems, yet they were still hesitant to do something about it. What if taking action against the doll made things worse? Paul knows it sounds silly now, but it made perfect sense to them back then. As if to confirm their suspicions, a scary incident happened one night when their adult son, Tom, came over to visit. Aware of the "haunted doll" situation, Tom asked his father what he was planning to do with it. Paul answered, "I suppose get rid of it." As soon as he said this, the lights in the house flickered. The men looked out the window and saw no signs of a power outage, prompting Tom to ask, somewhat jokingly, "You're sure you want to get rid of it?" Suddenly the house went completely dark. Paul and Tom, who were the only ones home at the time, nearly knocked each other over as they rushed out the front door. Minutes later, the lights came back on. The men passed each other a knowing look; there would be no further talk about the doll that evening.

Paul's reluctance to "do something" with the doll reached its limit a few weeks later when the doll crossed the threshold from creepy mischief into frightful violence. It was a Friday night and Terry was standing in front of a mirror getting dressed and putting on earrings before going out to dinner with Paul. About five feet away on her right side, a folded-up baby swing was leaning against an overstuffed chair. Behind the swing, on the cushion of the chair, sat the doll. Paul was on his way to the bedroom and could see Terry through the open door. What he saw next left him in shock. The swing flew up and slammed into Terry's side. Recalling the event several years later, Paul still couldn't believe what he had seen. "There was no way a baby swing, leaning against a chair, could get up and fly five feet in the air. It's impossible!" Terrified and in pain, Terry demanded that the doll be removed from the house. Paul didn't want to be alone with the doll in the outside darkness, so he temporarily locked it in a storage trunk at the end of their bed.

For the next several days, all was calm in the house. The family dared to hope that their problems with the doll were over. But then one night as Paul was close to falling asleep, the ashtray on his nightstand began spinning and rocking. He watched in amazement until it stopped, and then, even more amazingly, felt his body being pushed up from underneath the mattress. He knew he should have jumped out of bed, but he was too scared to move at that point. He endured several repetitions of being pushed up and left to drop before it finally stopped as mysteriously as it began. He looked over at Terry and was relieved to hear her snoring softly. Apparently, he was the only intended target of the phantom assault.

The next morning, Paul wasted no time. He grabbed the doll out of the trunk, stuffed her in a green plastic garbage bag, and put the bag in a dark corner of his shed at the far end of the backyard. There she remained for four years, behind old lawnmowers, broken gardening tools, and other discarded items, before Paul finally took her out to show to a paranormal investigator who was interviewing the family for a book project.

Paul admitted that he considered removing the doll completely from the property, but as time went on without any more trouble, he felt it best not to upset the status quo. He still vividly remembered the night the lights flashed on and off, as if the doll was trying to communicate with him. "Sometimes I think it was telling me, 'No! I don't want to go.'" After his interview, Paul put the doll back in the plastic bag, twisted it closed with a wire tie, and returned it to the far corner of the shed. Paul had no misgivings; she seemed content in there, and his family would soon forget she was even nearby.

Nonetheless, the snap of the padlock on the shed door was a comforting sound.

79

CHAPTER 7

The Jersey Devil

Though it's now sixty-some years in the past, Michael Orfe still remembers the date he had in high school with a girl named Violet, but not for the usual reasons. Fun and romance were not the highlights of the evening, as Michael recalled in an episode of *Fox Nation's Monsters Across America*. Terror and disbelief were. Michael recounted driving his father's car down a dark, unpaved road in New Jersey's Pine Barrens, feeling, as he put it, "comfortable and cocky," when suddenly Violet thought she saw something ahead of them. Michael slowed the car and rolled down the windows. Though he didn't see anything right away, he definitely sensed "there was something out in the woods, in the pines." Moments later, Violet let out a gut-wrenching scream. A large clawed hand was coming through her window, right toward her head. Michael lunged over and started rolling up the window, trapping the hideous-looking arm and cutting into it until blood began to spurt on the couple's faces. Panic-stricken, Michael tried to put the car in gear, but the momentary confusion allowed their attacker to pull free from the window, leap up onto the hood, and shatter the windshield with a thunderous blow of his arm. Michael finally managed to put the car in reverse, which sent the creature tumbling off the hood into the scrubby pine growth. Not daring to look back, Michael turned the car around and drove like a bat out of hell to the nearest ranger station. After reporting their terrifying encounter, a ranger accompanied the couple back out to the scene where, in addition to finding blood in the road, they found footprints leading to the woods. Oddly, only the right print looked somewhat human. The left was in the shape of a cloven hoof.

Michael Orfe is convinced he and his girlfriend had encountered the infamous Jersey Devil that warm summer night decades ago, a creature that has been the subject of New Jersey folklore for nearly 300 years. Most commonly described as having the body of a kangaroo, the head of a dog, the face of a horse, bat wings, cloven feet, horns, talons, and a tail, the Jersey Devil is said to roam the region of south Jersey known as the Pine Barrens, a one million acre reserve of dark forests and swampy bogs.

According to legend, the origin of the Jersey Devil came about in 1735, when a destitute woman known as Mother Leeds found herself pregnant with her 13th child. Distraught by the pregnancy and the living conditions in which her drunkard husband left her and the other 12 children, she raised her hands to the heavens and proclaimed, "I am tired of children. Let this one be a devil!" Months later, during a tumultuous storm, Mother Leeds prepared to give birth with the assistance of several midwives who had gathered around her while her husband and other children waited in an adjoining room. The birth went well, and all present, including Mother Leeds, seemed happy to welcome a normal-looking baby boy to the world. But suddenly the infant began to transform into something hideous. Its body elongated into a serpentine shape while its face grew long and bony like a horse. Bat wings grew from its shoulders, horns sprouted from its head, and claws ripped through once-delicate baby fingertips. Its eyes glowed red and its forked tail whipped back and forth as it grew to an impossible size before the astonished onlookers.

At this point, the accounts differ as to what happened next. Some have the creature simply escaping through the chimney. Others have it going up the chimney but only after beating those present with its wings and tail. The most horrifying accounts have it killing everyone in the house, including Mother Leeds, before it smashed its way up and out the chimney, leaving a pile of rubble in its wake. Regardless of the amount of carnage attributed to its "birth," the accounts do agree that the devil creature disappeared into the desolation and darkness of the Pine Barrens, where it has lived ever since.

Sightings and run-ins with the "Leeds Devil," as it was often called, began soon after that stormy night, with local residents claiming to hear its blood-curling shrieks in the still of the night, and blaming everything from dead farm animals to failed crops on the cursed creature's presence. Even some famous historical figures have turned up in Jersey Devil lore. In the early 1800s, American naval hero Commodore Stephen Decatur was said to be testing cannonballs at the Hanover Iron Works range in the Pines when he spotted a bizarre creature flapping its wings over the range. He immediately fired a cannonball at the beast, hitting it squarely, according to witness accounts. Amazingly, the direct hit didn't seem to faze the creature at all as it continued flying past the speechless onlookers. And in 1820, Joseph Bonaparte, former King of Spain and brother of Napoleon, claimed to have seen the Devil while hunting near his estate in Bordentown, New Jersey.

Stories of the Devil continued throughout the 19th century. In 1840, a widespread slaughter of sheep and chickens was attributed to the creature, with locals reporting hearing awful screams and finding strange tracks at the scenes of the killings. Posses were organized but always failed to find the murderous culprit. In 1858, W.F. Mayer of New York came to the Pine Barrens for an article he was writing for the *Atlantic Monthly*. He interviewed over 50 local residents and was amazed at the prevalent fear of the Devil they were convinced lived in their midst. Mayer wrote that many Pines residents refused to go out after dark. Sightings continued throughout the late 1800s in various Pine Barrens communities, including Haddonfield, Bridgeton, Smithville, Long Beach Island, and Leeds Point. In the 1880s, hysteria in one community prompted the report that the Devil "carried off anything that moved." In 1899, the Devil supposedly flew up north to the New Jersey-New York border and was spotted near a bridge over the Pascack River, and later near a rock in Hyenga Lake. Word quickly got around that an unusual creature was haunting the area that could "fly, swim, and run like a deer."

But it was 1909 that truly became "The Year of the Jersey Devil." During the week of January 16 through 23, thousands of people reported seeing the winged creature throughout the Delaware Valley, with sightings reported not just in small towns and villages but also in the major cities of Philadelphia and Camden. Descriptions of the beast were as colorful as they were varied: "kangaroo horse," "flying death," "woozlebug," "cowbird," "flying horse," and "prehistoric lizard" were just some of the names used by terrified witnesses. By the end of the week, the hysteria had grown so large that schools throughout southern New Jersey and the Philadelphia area were either closed or experienced low attendance. Mills in the Pine Barrens were forced to close when workers refused to walk through the woods to their jobs.

Residents who didn't see the Devil itself had a good chance of at least seeing its footprints. They were so numerous in the fresh-fallen snow that covered the region that the Asbury Park Press carried a story about it, with its headline reading: "What Mysterious Tracks are These? Jersey Fields and Yards Covered by Imprints of a Two-Legged Something." The tracks were mysterious indeed, defying every logical explanation as to their existence. They led across fields, through backyards, over and under fences, climbed up trees, jumped from rooftop to rooftop, and disappeared as suddenly as they appeared. Adding to the enigma, the size of the tracks varied, with some being as large as horse's hooves, and others mere inches in length. One thing was consistent, though: they weren't human. In rural Burlington County, a group of men organized a hunt for the creature and brought in bloodhounds to lead the way. The dogs, however, refused to follow the tracks, leaving the men to go off on their own for about four miles before the footprints mysteriously ended.

Patrolman James Sackville of the Bristol Police Department was one of the first witnesses to lay eyes on the creature. He was making his rounds in the early morning hours of Sunday the 16th when barking dogs led him down a dark street. There he came face to face with what he described as a winged beast with the features of some sort of peculiar animal. He drew his revolver and ran toward it, prompting the creature to hop like a bird in retreat while emitting a terrible scream. Officer Sackville fired several shots at the thing, but to no effect, as it soon spread its wings and flew off into the night. At around the same time, the Postmaster of Bristol, E.W. Minster, was looking out his window while dealing with a bout of insomnia when he saw what was most likely the same creature fleeing from Officer Sackville. It was flying over the Delaware River and "emitting a glow like a firefly." Minster went on to describe it as having the head of a ram, with curled horns, long wings, short front legs, and longer back legs, all the while uttering a high, piercing shriek.

All week long, reports of the fearsome creature echoed throughout the region. A husband and wife in Gloucester City were awakened by strange noises they said came from a creature cavorting on the top of their shed. Three-and-a-half feet in height, with the head of a dog and the face of a horse, the thing pranced about on its hind legs for ten minutes before giving a final bark and flying off into the night. A meeting of the Black Hawk Social Club in Camden was interrupted when an "uncanny sound" drew members' attention to a back window. There, peering back at them, was a gruesome, inhuman face that made the attendees flee in terror. Shortly thereafter, in the area of Haddon Heights, it appeared before a trolley car full of passengers. "There's that thing!" one passenger bellowed out. It followed the car for about 200 yards, circling above it with its wings spread wide until it gave a loud hiss and flew out of sight. Witnesses described the creature as a flying kangaroo. In Burlington, another trolley car full of passengers saw the beast as it scurried across the tracks in front of the car.

In West Collingswood, two men were walking down the street when they saw what looked like an ostrich on the roof of the fire chief's house. They called the fire department and soon a crew of firemen was firing water hoses at the strange intruder. Not liking the water, it jumped off the roof and ran down the street for a short distance before turning back and suddenly charging its tormentors. Just before it bore down on the terrified crowd, it spread its wings and soared over them, disappearing into the night.

The winged marauder also caused havoc with livestock in the region, with numerous reports coming in of missing and slaughtered chickens. Curiously, many of the chickens were found dead with no marks on them, leading farmers to wonder if they were choked or died of fright. Though tracks were left at the locations—some so numerous "it looked like a herd of Shetland ponies had stampeded there in the dark"—they always failed to lead to a viable suspect.

Apparently tired of chickens, the Devil was later seen in south Camden trying out a new delicacy. Hearing commotion in her backyard, Mrs. Mary Sorbinski hurried out to find her beloved little dog in the clutches of a "horrible monster." In a desperate attempt to save her pet, Mrs. Sorbinski flailed at the beast with a broom until it finally let go of the dog and flew away. In a state of panic and shock, Mrs. Sorbinski screamed for help as she held the near-lifeless, mangled body of her pet. A large crowd soon gathered at her house, but their low-level murmurs were quickly overshadowed by uncanny shrieks that came from a street over. Two policemen in the throng raced to the sounds, followed closely by the rest of the crowd. Seeing a dark, inhuman-looking figure on top of a hill, they emptied their revolvers at it, but to no avail. Once again proving itself incapable of capture, the Devil spread its wings and disappeared into the night, leaving the officers and other witnesses frozen in disbelief.

The week of terror ended as suddenly as it started, with only one other sighting of the creature reported in 1909. Nonetheless, the brief but intense rampage experienced throughout the Delaware Valley, and reported on the front pages of city newspapers, forever changed the image of the "Leeds Devil." No longer was it regarded as just an old wives' tale whispered about in the Pine Barrens; it had now become a newsworthy threat that everyone throughout the region was referring to as the Jersey Devil.

While reports of the Devil died down considerably since that wintry week in 1909, encounters happened consistently enough to keep the legend alive and flourishing. In 1927, a taxi driver on his way to Salem, New Jersey, was forced to pull over on a deserted rural road to fix a flat tire. He had just finished with the repair when suddenly the cab began shaking violently from side to side. Looking up, the driver was astonished to see "something that stood upright like a man but without clothing and covered with hair." Leaving his jack and flat tire in the road, the driver jumped in the car and drove full speed to Salem.

On July 28, 1937, the *Philadelphia Evening Bulletin* reported how numerous locals claimed to have seen a creature with glowing red eyes lurking around the outskirts of Downingtown. Cydney Ladley, along with his wife and another neighbor, told of seeing the beast on a back road near his home. "It leaped across the road in front of my car," said Ladley. "It was about the size of a kangaroo, was covered with hair four inches long, and it hopped like a kangaroo. And eyes! What eyes!"

In 1951 in Gibbstown, New Jersey, a 10-year-old boy began screaming hysterically, claiming he saw "the thing" outside a window with blood all over its face. Over the next couple of days, dozens of other people in the area reported either hearing "unearthly screams" or seeing a fearsome, inhuman creature. The number of calls placed to the police during that time became unmanageable, prompting the chief of police to officially declare the Jersey Devil sightings a hoax and to place signs saying as much around the outskirts of town to keep out curious tourists.

One of the more gruesome events attributed to the Devil happened in April 1966, when Steven Silkotch awoke and discovered that a massacre had occurred the night before at his farm. Strewn about the grounds were the mauled and ravished remains of thirty-one ducks, three geese, four cats, and two large dogs. One of the dogs, a 90-pound German Shepherd, had been dragged a quarter of a mile from the killing scene. New Jersey State Police were called in to investigate, and while they did find a number of large tracks, they were unable to determine for certain what had slaughtered Silkotch's livestock.

The rise of social media in the new millennium has kept the Jersey Devil as relevant as any other titillating subject of legend and lore. Paranormal discussion sites and comment sections attached to evergreen articles about New Jersey's flagship monster are filled with stories from people claiming to have seen or heard the mysterious creature. Every so often a photo is shared purporting to be proof of the Devil's existence. One such popular image from a trail cam shows a strange winged creature running on four legs after a frightened deer. Another, from 2015, made a viral splash online and was even picked up by the major news networks. It was taken by security guard David Black near a golf course in Galloway. Black was driving home from work when he saw what appeared to be a llama running through the trees lining the road. When the "llama" suddenly spread a pair of wings and flew up over the golf course, Black stopped the car and grabbed his cell phone. The image he captured left him dumbfounded. He sent the photo to *NJ.com*, hoping someone could help him figure out what he just saw. "Either my mind is playing tricks on me or I just saw the Jersey Devil," he wrote to the news outlet. As quickly as the photo made the rounds on the Internet, its authenticity just as quickly took a hit when follow-up efforts to contact Black proved futile and the photo itself fell prey to scathing reviews by amateur and professional debunkers alike.

Attempts to explain what the Jersey Devil actually is have been as successful as trying to explain Bigfoot. But there is no shortage of theories. Perhaps it's a prehistoric creature that somehow survived the passage of time. Perhaps it's a deformed animal or large bird such as the Sand Hill Crane, which is known to act aggressively when confronted. Perhaps the sightings are incidents of mass hysteria or the result of clever pranksters. Maybe a combination of both. Then, of course, maybe it's exactly what the old timers claimed it was: Mother Leeds's devil child. The curse that Mother Leeds uttered, according to some paranormal theorists, could have resulted in bringing about a paranormal creature, much as curses can bring about poltergeist activity and other dark energies.

Though residents may disagree as to *what* is out there in the New Jersey wilderness, there is a common belief that *something* is out there. Be it a monstrous entity that roams the mist-shrouded marshes or a fearsome fantasy that haunts the collective unconscious of the local population, the Jersey Devil exists in one form or another. Skeptics are invited to spend the night alone in the Pine Barrens to decide which it might be.

CHAPTER 8

The Furry Phantom

In the spring of 1979, having just received a medical discharge from the British Army, Andrew Taylor moved into a small flat in Edinburgh that his close friends, Kevin and Lyle, had been leasing for about two months. The basement rental was far from inviting, with bars on the windows, creaky floorboards, and a dampness that permeated the walls. But Andrew only planned on staying until he could find a place of his own. In the meantime, he could put up with cramped conditions and a little cold. What Andrew didn't know at the time was that the flat had another occupant, one that was not nearly as welcoming as his friends.

Andrew's first inkling that there was something odd afoot occurred when he was alone one afternoon soon after moving in. As he made his way down the dark, narrow hallway to the kitchen to make a cup of tea, he couldn't shake the feeling, as silly as it seemed, that he wasn't truly alone. He started to fill the tea kettle with water, when suddenly he heard a voice close to his right ear blurt out, "Yes?" Andrew spun around, sloshing water everywhere, but faced only an empty kitchen. Thinking that perhaps one of his roommates came home early, he searched the flat but found only the cat, huddled and hissing under the sink with its hackles raised.

About a week later, Andrew heard the voice again, but this time he wasn't alone. Kevin and his girlfriend, Jane, had just returned from a shopping trip and joined Andrew in the living room to put their feet up and chat. After a bit, Jane excused herself, at which time Andrew decided to tell Kevin about the voice he'd heard in the kitchen. Kevin listened with interest, even a bit pensively, as if he had a story of his own to share. He yelled out to Jane to put the kettle on; a cup of tea was definitely in order. "Yes," a voice answered back. Andrew knew instantly that the voice wasn't Jane's. It was, in fact, the same voice he had heard last week. He jumped up and led Kevin into the kitchen, which was, once again, empty. The two friends stood in stunned silence until their attention was turned to the front door opening. In walked Jane, who had gone back to the grocer after discovering she had forgotten something earlier.

That night, Kevin and Lyle admitted to Andrew that odd things had been happening in the flat before he moved in. It started with strange noises, in particular that of a baby crying. The sound would start softly and gradually increase in volume until the whole flat was reverberating. Then it would abruptly stop. The sound of labored breathing was also common and would often follow the men around the flat, especially in the middle of the night when they would awake to use the bathroom. Then there was the matter of objects disappearing one day and reappearing another in strange locations. Lyle recalled putting his watch down on his nightstand one morning while dressing and finding it missing when he went to put it on. Two days later, he found the watch in a cookie tin in the pantry.

Rattled by the unseen presence in their midst, the men started sleeping in the same room. One night, a warm furry animal jumped on top of Kevin's bed. Assuming it was the cat, he began petting and talking softly to it as it purred. Lyle yelled over to him to quit talking to himself. The cat was with *him*. A mutual friend who was crashing with them that night spoke up and told them both to be quiet, as *he* had the cat. Kevin immediately jumped up and turned on a light, which revealed three bewildered humans but no cat anywhere in sight.

After hearing his roommates' stories, Andrew was a bit miffed they hadn't mentioned any of this before now. Then again, he could understand how they didn't want to come across as looking foolish, or make Andrew think they were trying to scare him from moving in. They all agreed to keep each other apprised of any unusual activity from that point on. It didn't take long before there were new things to talk about.

About two weeks later, in the middle of a warm July night, Andrew felt a small furry body jump into bed with him and curl up behind his head. Annoyed by the creature's heavy breathing on his neck, Andrew turned over to shoo it away, thinking it was the cat. What he found, however, was nothing furry or four-footed, either in his bed or in his room. Lyle's and Kevin's story of their phantom cat came instantly to his mind.

The following Saturday, Kevin awoke just before 5:00 a.m. and found himself on his stomach, unable to turn over. In fact, he couldn't move at all. Suddenly, the bed began vibrating, little by little until it was violently rocking from side to side. Terrified, he tried to call out, but found his voice was paralyzed as well. His other senses still working, he felt something heavy jump up on the shaking bed and crawl toward his head. It rubbed its furry body all along him and breathed into his face, its breath wet and putrid. Kevin thought he was going to pass out. Then, as suddenly as it started, the shaking ended, the foul-smelling hairy thing was gone, and Kevin could move again. He stumbled out of bed to look for his flatmates, but they were both still sleeping. Outside the living room window, he spotted their cat looking in. Its ears were flat and its teeth were bared. It refused to enter the flat for days.

After these events, the men decided to sleep in the same bedroom again. They had retired for the night and were discussing what to do about their unwanted lodger when they heard heavy footsteps in the living room. They had closed and locked the bedroom door, but Andrew jumped up anyway and pushed a chair up under the door handle. Moments later, the doorknob started to turn and the door began to bend inwards as if something huge was pushing against it from the other side. The men watched in fear as the twisting and pushing action was repeated three times. Then it stopped and the footsteps retreated toward the kitchen. They heard the kitchen door open and slam shut, and then silence. Andrew recalled that they were all too shaken to investigate. Thankfully, nothing else happened that night.

In fact, nothing else happened for a month after the strange intruder came calling at their door. Hoping that whatever had been terrorizing them had perhaps left for good, the roommates got back to their normal routines of studying, working, and partying. One night in August, after a late-night students' party a few miles away, Lyle came home with his girlfriend and the two settled into Lyle's makeshift bedroom, which at the time was a curtained-off part of the dining room. Just as he was about to fall into a deep sleep, something caught Lyle's attention and he snapped fully awake. The kitchen door was opening . . . but no one was on the other side. His girlfriend was also now awake and the two of them watched as the door slowly opened and closed several times on its own until it finally stayed open. Lyle got out of bed to close and lock it, but as he reached for it, the door slammed shut with a thundering bang. Lyle's girlfriend informed him the next morning that she was never entering the flat again.

A week later, Lyle was awakened once again by a door opening, but this time when he looked he saw Kevin coming in the front door followed closely by his girlfriend Jane. After sitting up and groggily accepting a cup of tea Kevin offered him, Lyle looked around and asked where Jane was. Surprised by the question, Kevin answered that Jane was at school and would be all day.

By this point, Andrew was determined to find an explanation for the strange goings-on. He convinced his roommates to participate in a séance. Perhaps if they could make contact with the entity in the flat, he reasoned, they could figure out what to do about it. So, on a Saturday morning in late August, Andrew, Kevin, Lyle, and their friend, Brian, gathered around the kitchen table and placed their hands on a Ouija board that Andrew had picked up at an occult bookshop. "Is anybody there?" Andrew asked, opening the session. Nothing answered him, nor did anything answer Kevin or Brian when they asked. But when Lyle asked, the planchette shot to the word YES. Lyle continued the questioning, during which the "spirit" claimed to be a French businessman who died of an illness in the building. He was looking for peace, he said, but when pressed would give no more information.

Andrew wasn't satisfied. For one thing, he felt there were multiple entities in the flat, given the varied amount of paranormal activity they had all experienced. He persuaded his friends to do another séance, this one four days later at midnight. The participants were the same, but with the addition of two female students. This time it was Brian who made contact, but it was with a different spirit. This one claimed to be from another time dimension, the 21st century. When asked why it would only respond to Brian, the spirit answered that Brian was his ancestor. It also said it was trapped in their time zone and wanted out.

The absurdity of the session was too much for Kevin, and he jokingly asked, "How much is petrol going for in the future?" All at once, the planchette flew across the table, the lights went out, and the kitchen door closed by itself. The two female students screamed while the men tried to open the door to no avail. For several moments, but for what seemed an eternity, chaos ensued in the small abode. Then, as if by magic, the lights flashed back on and the door released its hold. The girls rushed out of the flat, screaming hysterically the entire way.

During the melee, the flat had dropped to an icy cold temperature and it stayed that way through the night. Unable to sleep and wrestling with a growing sense of foreboding, Andrew was still awake at 3:00 a.m. when he heard a loud crash in the kitchen, followed by the sound of the table being dragged across the floor and objects being thrown about. The cacophony lasted about 10 minutes, but Andrew stayed in bed even after it ended. He had no desire to see, or feel, the source of the bedlam. The next morning, Kevin admitted he heard the sounds too. The two men cautiously entered the kitchen together, only to find nothing out of place.

That very day, Lyle packed up and left. Kevin left two weeks later and moved into a flat with Jane. Not wanting to be alone in the basement, Andrew arranged to temporarily share an upper room with a young cook. For two weeks, all was calm except for the occasional sound of footsteps ascending the staircase in the hall. Then one night around 2:00 a.m., Andrew came home from a night out with friends. As he entered the dark building, a sense of foreboding returned. He felt along the wall for the light to the stairwell, anxious to get into his flat, when something cold and furry grabbed his hand. Andrew shrieked and bolted up the unlit stairs. As he fumbled with his key, he ventured a look behind him. Staring up at him from the inky darkness at the bottom of the stairs were two slitted yellow eyes.

From that night forward, Andrew slept very little. Whatever unseen presence had been haunting the basement had moved to the top floor and wouldn't leave him alone. Strange noises at all hours of the night. Cabinet doors creaking open by themselves. Personal items going missing. It quickly proved to be too much. Andrew moved out as soon as he could and never set eyes on the building again. He was too afraid of what might be looking back.

CHAPTER 9

The Black-Eyed Kids

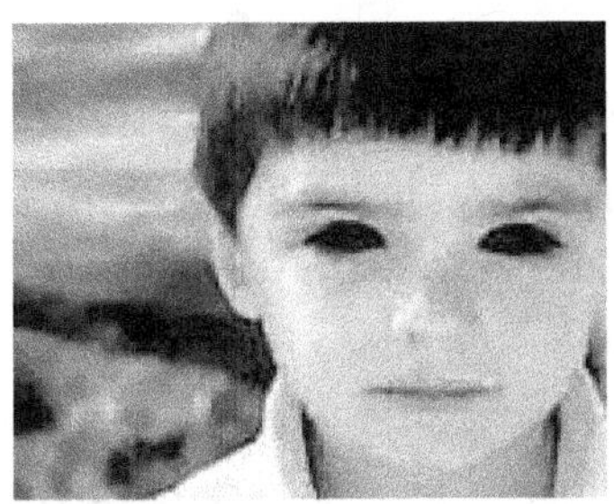

Sara was a bit surprised at the light traffic at her house this Halloween. Her neighborhood in this part of north Texas was usually a trick-or-treat mecca, attracting even a lot of non-neighbor kids who were dropped off at one end of the street and picked up at the other. Sara and her husband weren't complaining, though. The quiet night suited them as they watched television and waited for their teenage son to return from a party. At about 9:30, not having had any more kids at the door for over a half hour, they turned off the porch light and let their bulldog, Chloe, out of her crate. At 10:00, Sara's husband announced he was too tired to stay up any longer and went upstairs, while Sara curled up on the couch with Chloe, intending to keep watching ghost shows until her son got home.

A few minutes later, there was a knock at the door. *Really?* thought Sara. *This late?* She considered ignoring it, but she also knew that she was visible to the visitor through the beveled glass window on the door. She stood up and wondered why Chloe wasn't racing over there like she usually does when someone's at the door. *Knock, knock, knock.* That got the dog moving, but to Sara's astonishment, Chloe ran *out* of the living room, away from the door. She thought about yelling for her husband, but she could hear the shower running and knew he wouldn't hear her. Just then, the light from a passing car illuminated her front door window just enough to see two small children standing outside. While she felt relief that it was probably just neighbor kids, she also wondered what parents were allowing their children out that late by themselves.

She opened the door just a crack in case Chloe decided to come back and try to escape. She was immediately struck by the fact that the kids, a girl and a boy, weren't wearing costumes and didn't say "trick or treat." In fact, they didn't say anything at all at first. They were standing far enough back that Sara couldn't make out their distinct features, but she could tell that the girl was a bit older, maybe 11 or 12, with long blonde hair, and the boy was around 8 or 9, with short brown hair. Sara was about to ask them what they were doing here when the girl spoke: "Ma'am, can we please come inside and use your phone to call our mom?" A deep feeling of unease began to arise in Sara. Something wasn't right. She fumbled for words. "Um, hon, don't you have a phone of your own?" The girl and boy looked at each other for several seconds before turning back to Sara. "My cell phone battery doesn't have any charge left in it. Can we please come inside and call our mother? We're alone out here and my brother is scared."

As much as Sara wanted to follow her maternal instincts and let them in, her gut was telling her something completely different. She noticed that she had unknowingly opened the door a bit further and found herself fighting the urge to open it more. She then told the girl to give her the number and that she would call her mom herself. Again, the children looked at each other silently for several moments. Then, turning back to Sara, the girl said, "Ma'am, my little brother has to use the bathroom. Can we please come inside while you call our mom?" As she said this, the girl walked closer to the door, almost like she expected to walk right in. That's when Sara saw her face clearly—and nearly passed out from fright. The girl's eyes were jet black, from top to bottom and side to side. Sara immediately closed the door to a crack, stopping the girl's forward pace. The girl pleaded more vehemently: "Please, we HAVE to come inside. We're scared and alone. Please help us!" Then, as if acting out a well-rehearsed script, both children started crying and whimpering.

Sara slammed the door shut and locked it, fear overriding any other emotions. "I'll call your mother if you give me her number, but I'm not letting you in," she said in a loud voice. While keeping one eye on the door, she quickly ran over and grabbed her phone off the table. Only when she started to call her neighbor across the street did she see the kids move from her porch to under a streetlight on the boulevard. They continued to stare at her through the door until she actually put the phone to her ear and started talking. Then they slowly started walking down the street. Moments later, Sara and her neighbor met by the streetlight, but no children were anywhere to be seen.

Sara's story is rather typical in the annals of "Black-Eyed Kids" (BEK) encounters. Most of the witness testimonies feature children ranging from age 6 to 16 mysteriously showing up at someone's home or vehicle and insisting on being let inside. Often speaking in a monotone voice, sometimes using "old-fashioned" or formal speech, they will ask to use the telephone or the bathroom. If it's a car they're at, they'll ask for a ride. Refuse them and they'll get more verbally forceful, pleading that they *must* come in, they *need* to come in, that it's an emergency of some sort. People who encounter them almost immediately feel a sense of dread or even outright terror, along with a hypnotic-like urge to comply with their demands. But the scariest thing about these children is their eyes. They are completely blacked out, nothing but deep black orbs devoid of sclera or iris.

Reports of beings with black eyes are nothing new in the legends and lore of humankind. But the torrent of black-eyed kid encounters that have been recorded over the last few decades are unique, both for their similarities and for their level of creepiness. Unlike some paranormal phenomena that have become a part of popular culture, the start of BEK sightings can be traced back to a specific place and time by a seemingly reliable source. Journalist Brian Bethel, a reporter for the *Abilene Reporter-News*, had something incredible happen to him in 1996 and wanted to write about it yet not lose his credibility. So he posted his story on an Internet group site. After receiving positive responses, and even corroborating accounts from people all over the world, Bethel retold his story on the TV show *Monsters and Mysteries in America* in 2012, and wrote about his experience again in the *Abilene Reporter-News* in 2013. His story goes like this:

Brian needed to pay his Internet service provider's bill. In the days before automated bill pay, it was still necessary to write checks and deliver them physically. So Brian drove from his apartment to downtown Abilene, where a drop box for Camalott Communications was located. He pulled into an empty parking space and began writing out a check, using the light of a neighboring movie theater's marquee to see. Suddenly, there was a knock on the driver's side window that made him jump. Standing alongside his car and staring at him were two young boys between the ages of 9 and 12. Boy number one had an olive complexion, curly brown hair, and wore a gray hooded shirt and jeans. "He exuded an air of quiet confidence," Brian recalled. Boy number two had pale skin and seemed nervous. He was dressed in a green hooded pullover and had light-colored hair. Brian's first thought was that they were a couple of homeless kids who were going to hit him up for money. But then "the air changed" and Brian felt this overwhelming sense of fear and unearthliness overtake him. Boy number one smiled, which for some reason sent a chill up Brian's spine. Nonetheless, Brian rolled the window down and asked, "Yes?"

Still smiling with very white teeth showing, the boy answered, "Hey, mister, we have a problem. My friend and I want to see a film but we forgot our money. We need to go to our house to get it. Want to help us out?" In his job as a reporter, Brian had interacted with many kids over the years. What struck him about this one was not only his calm and unwavering diction but, primarily, his adult-like boldness that Brian had to admit had a certain seductive quality to it. He fumbled with a response. "Uh, well . . ." That response didn't appear to set well with the boys. They seemed perturbed, as if Brian should have opened the car door by now. The older one pressed again. "C'mon, mister. We just want to go to our house. And we're just two little boys."

Every feeler in his body and brain told Brian that something about these boys was "wrong." He struggled again to find words before finally asking, "What movie were you going to see?"

"*Mortal Kombat*, of course," Boy One said smoothly. Boy Two nodded in agreement. Brian glanced over at the theater's marquee and saw that the last showing of *Mortal Kombat* had started an hour earlier. "C'mon, mister. Let us in. We can't get in your car until you do, you know. Just let us in, and we'll be gone before you know it. We'll go to our mother's house."

Horrified that his hand had started to stray toward the door lock, Brian snapped to attention and violently pulled it away. Then, for the first time since the encounter started, he locked eyes with the boys. What he saw he'll never forget. Coal black orbs, no pupils, no irises, that shimmered in the half-light of the marquee. Looks of anger flashed across the boys' faces. *They know I'm on to them*, thought Brian.

"C'mon, mister," the oldest pleaded more insistently. "We won't hurt you. You have to LET US IN."

That was enough for Brian. He rolled up the window and gripped the gearshift, prompting the speaking boy to bang on the window and wail: "We can't come in unless you tell us it's okay. Let . . . us . . . in!" At that, Brian peeled into reverse and tore out of the parking lot. Mere moments later, he glanced back. The boys were gone.

What exactly *are* these mysterious, intimidating, and all-together creepy black-eyed beings? Are they really just children wearing black contacts or high on some hallucinatory drug that dilates their pupils? Probably not, as the scores of witness reports describe words and actions by these kids not consistent with typical narcotic use. And black contacts that cover the entire eye, including the sclera (the whites), are not only prohibitively expensive for most kids but would likely be very uncomfortable to wear, especially for younger children.

If not actual human children, then what? There is some thought that they are human-alien hybrid beings, a theory that stems from witness and abductee stories of humanoid, long-limbed aliens with large, jet-black, almond-shaped eyes, popularly referred to as "Grays" in the UFO community. Others think they may be from this planet but from an alternate dimension, which would explain their ability to disappear so quickly. The mystical-minded have speculated they are members of the Fae, preternatural beings who coexist with humans but prefer to live hidden and apart, and who communicate primarily telepathically. Then there is the more traditional belief that they are evil supernatural entities that disguise themselves in human form, take over existing human bodies, or are actual demons from Hell itself.

One of the more popular theories bandied about suggests that these beings are a type of vampire, not the cinematic version that sucks the blood from its prey, but rather an otherworldly entity that feeds by draining the life-force energy from its victims. In his book *Paranormal Parasites*, author Nick Redfern tells of several BEK encounters that seem to support this belief. One particularly chilling account revolves around an Oklahoma truck driver, Martin, who was looking forward to relaxing at home for a few days after a long stint on the road. At around 8:30 on his first night home, Martin heard a knock on his door. Assuming it was his neighbor, Martin threw open the door and was surprised to see a boy and a girl, both around 11 or 12 years old, holding hands and staring at him with eerie-looking large black eyes. The boy was wearing a black hoodie and the girl a black top with jeans. They appeared sickly to Martin, but also something else: dangerous. The girl spoke and told Martin they were homeless and needed something to eat. When interviewed later about the encounter, Martin stated that he felt transfixed by their stares and unable to close the door, which he knew he should have done as soon as he saw their hideous eyes. The girl repeated, "We need to eat. May we come in?" Amazingly, Martin did invite them in, but he recalled it happening in a dreamlike sequence. The next thing he remembered, he was sitting on the couch with the two children standing in front of him. The girl said one word: *eat*.

All of a sudden, Martin felt like he was starving, as if he hadn't eaten in days. Yet, he had no way of helping himself. He was weak and ill-feeling, barely unable to keep his head up, let alone stand and walk to the kitchen. As the children continued to stare intently at him, and as he continued to grow weaker and weaker, Martin suddenly had a terrifying realization: they were using him for food. Surprisingly, and thankfully, the ordeal didn't last long, and after a few minutes the children turned and left, holding hands like when they arrived. Martin finally managed to crawl to his bedroom, where he fell into a deep sleep. He remained in bed for three days, where he continued to experience overwhelming weakness, bouts of dizziness, and a strange, unpleasant taste in his mouth. It took a full week before he felt well enough to get back on the road. On the move and ever vigilant for the paranormal predators that now haunt his dreams.

Martin's case is unusual in that most BEKs never actually get inside the house or car of their intended target, as their appearance and "bad vibes" usually scare the homeowner into slamming the door or the driver into racing away before any further contact—physical or mental—can be completed. Another thing that has probably saved more than one person from becoming a victim, and not merely a witness, is the unwritten rule the children seem to follow that keeps them from crossing a threshold until given consent. They certainly try hard to gain that consent, generally going from asking to imploring to *demanding* to be let in, but there is no record of them forcibly entering someone's domain.

Another, but less reported, trait of BEKs is their use of "older" language. This was something that struck Martin when the girl said, "May we come in?" instead of the more common expression "can we?" This next account takes that peculiarity to a whole new level.

Josh was up late with his baby daughter so that his wife, a nurse who worked a 4:00 a.m. starting shift, could get some sleep. He had been watching YouTube videos, but when he found himself getting drowsy, he turned off the laptop and lay down on the spare bed in the baby's room. Just as he started dosing off, he heard a thumping noise on the front porch that startled him awake. Thinking it was their cat jumping around or scratching itself, Josh let himself dose off again. *Thump, thump, thump.* This time he got up and checked the porch. There was no one there. No cat either. He decided to make some tea and finish watching his videos as long as he was awake. As he sat there at the table, his attention was drawn to the kitchen window, where he saw two small-in-stature figures pass by under the curtain line. Then, on the back door, *knock, knock, knock.*

Irritated now that nuisance kids were out at 2:00 in the morning and were about to wake his sleeping wife and baby, Josh raced over to the door to catch the little delinquents. But as he threw open the door, the angry words he had been rehearsing in his mind suddenly stuck in his throat. In front of him were two 10-or-11-year-old boys, standing as still as stone, and staring at him with impenetrable pitch-black eyes. The repugnant odor of mold and a crushing feeling of dread made Josh suddenly nauseous, and he had to grip the door tighter to remain upright. One of the boys spoke: "May we use your telegraph?" The boy's strange request only added to Josh's addled condition. Did he hear right? Telegraph? Not telephone or cellphone? Confusion and apprehension running through him, he could only respond, "Huh?" The boy asked again to use the "telegraph." Wanting, *needing,* to get rid of them, Josh finally found words and said, "I don't have service at my house. Sorry." As he finished his sentence, he could see rage spread across their faces. He immediately closed and locked the door and then went to check on his daughter. Thankfully, he never saw the boys again.

Once they are gone, BEKs seem to be gone for good. It's almost as if they know they only have one chance of "tricking" a potential victim to let them in. After that, the game is up, so to speak. In this next account, the interaction between the black-eyed beings and their targets indeed resembles a game—a game of cat and mouse. In some respects, it is unique in BEK lore because it takes place over an extended period of time and at different locations. But at the end of the chase, it becomes the typical attempt at supplication and subversion.

Cal and Susan were enjoying a double date with their good friends, Greg and Kathy, on a pleasant Seattle evening. They had just left their favorite seafood restaurant and were on their way to their car when they noticed a group of four teenage boys watching them from the park across the street. Susan asked Cal if he knew them. Puzzled, Cal said no, why would he? Susan answered that they seemed to know him, as they were waving and one of them, she thought, called out Cal's name. Greg nervously eyed the group and urged his friends to get moving. The boys could be sizing them up for a robbery, he warned.

They got in their car, and as Cal backed out of the parking space, he made eye contact with one of the boys. And wished he hadn't. "His eyes were like black marbles," he stated later in an interview. "When I glanced at the other boys, they, too, seemed to have no ordinary pupils. Just black marbles." He peeled out of the parking lot, prompting Susan and Kathy to kid him about being paranoid. The boys were probably just wearing sunglasses to look cool, they remarked.

The couple's next stop was a movie theater a few miles away. The film was good and made them forget about the boys at the restaurant. That is, until they came out of the theater and saw the four of them leaning against a building across the street. They were dumbfounded. How did those kids know what movie they were going to? And how did they get there? There didn't appear to be a car near them. Just then, the one who appeared to be the leader of the group smiled broadly and waved at them. At this point, even Susan's and Kathy's cheerfulness was gone. An ominous feeling filled the air, and once again the friends hurried to their car while keeping a watchful eye on their would-be pursuers. There was one more stop they wanted to make, a bar across town. "I was determined to get as far away from the teenaged terrors as possible," Cal recalled. "As I looked at them, I couldn't help thinking of Kiefer Sutherland and his vampire gang in the old movie *The Lost Boys*."

Greg and Cal spent the entire ride to the bar looking out the back window and rearview mirror for any sign of the teenagers. Satisfied that they hadn't been followed, the foursome tried to shake off their foreboding as they entered their destination. About an hour and a half later, decidedly more relaxed after a few drinks, the friends left the bar . . . and came to a sobering stop. The teens were sitting on the curb across the street. After their initial shock wore off, everyone started talking at once. Greg wanted to call the police, Susan wanted to go home, and Kathy began accusing Greg and Cal of hiring the teens as part of an elaborate hoax. Cal ushered everyone into the car, dropped off Greg and Kathy, and then went home with Susan. Susan was quiet and, Cal could tell, frightened. He had to admit, so was he.

They weren't home for more than five minutes when the doorbell rang. Cal knew before he even looked in the peephole who he was going to see, and he was right. Standing at the door was the teen who had waved at him, the apparent leader of the group. Sitting on the steps were the other three. All of them were focused on the door with their impossibly black eyes. Grabbing a baseball bat, Cal yelled out, "What do you want?"

"Open the door," said the teen.

Cal told him that wasn't going to happen and that he was about to call the police. The boy then said, "I need to make a telephone call. Can I use your phone? I'll be quick. We need to have someone come and pick us up."

Cal was adamant. "No!"

"Can we use your bathroom? Please let us come in to use your bathroom. We have to go bad. Just in and out. Okay?"

"No!"

"Can we get something to eat? We haven't eaten all day and we're starving. Just a little food, please?"

Cal, exasperated, yelled back, "No! Now leave before I call the police!" This only incited the teen to become louder and more insistent. Soon the other three boys joined him in an eerie, monotonous chant: "Let us in. We need food. Let us in!"

Unknown to Cal, Susan had called the police as soon as the teens showed up at their door. Within a few minutes, a patrol car rounded the corner of their block, but when Cal looked back at the steps, the boys were gone. "They vanished in the blink of an eye," Cal stated. He and Susan told the responding officers that a gang of wild teenagers had been pounding on their door but had run away when they saw the police car. Cal offered one last reflection on that night: "When the officers asked what they looked like, we gave accurate descriptions—except for the solid black eyes."

Winding up this examination of the black-eyed children phenomenon is a story that is worth noting for its date. It happened in the early 1950s, well before the Internet fueled the rampant spread of BEK sightings, many of which are no doubt copycatted pieces of fiction. Maybe this story is an original piece of fiction. Maybe not. It is intriguing nonetheless.

Sixteen-year-old Harold was walking home from a friend's house in rural Virginia when he spotted a small figure leaning against a fence as if waiting for someone. As he got nearer, Harold saw it was a boy a little younger than himself, but one he didn't recognize, which was odd considering everyone knew everyone in Harold's community. He spoke to the boy but received no response, not even a look. He asked the boy if he was all right. There was a silent pause and then the boy looked up and said, "I wanna go to your house. Take me to your house." A wave of terror swept through Harold as he met the boy's eyes. They were solid black. As much as Harold wanted to look away, he found himself transfixed by the strange and terrible orbs. He tried to shake himself loose from their grip and run as fast as he could to his house. But then, chillingly, the boy said, "Now don't you run away from me. You're gonna walk me to your house."

Harold had heard enough. He tore himself away from the hypnotic gaze and bolted down the road to his house. As he ran, he heard a blood-curdling scream behind him, which he later recalled reminded him of a bobcat's screech. Arriving home, Harold burst through the front door and frantically told his parents what he had just seen. Believing without a doubt that their son had encountered someone, or something, threatening and fearsome, his father grabbed a shotgun and went out looking for the "devil boy." But a thorough search of the area showed no trace of him anywhere. Harold's mother, thinking her son had indeed encountered the devil in disguise, brought him to the local pastor to have him blessed.

In all likelihood, we'll never know for sure the truth behind the black-eyed kids phenomenon. Are they all the same type of being? Do they have a single point of origin? Or are black eyes just so frightening to humans that multiple entities use them as a means to terrify and control? The biggest question, of course, is: are these accounts even true? The witnesses in the foregoing stories all swear that what they saw was real. Skeptics will have to decide for themselves should they have that opportunity when there's a knock at the door at night and a child's voice says, "Let us in."

CHAPTER 10

The Wolf Man

Bill Ramsey had just returned home from a Saturday afternoon at the movies, and like any nine-year-old boy who had just watched several hours of heroic Royal Air Force fighter pilots save London from enemy German bombers, he was eager to play-act what was fresh in his mind. It was a lovely sunny day in 1952 in the seaside town of Southend, England, and Bill was having a great time playing fighter pilot alone in the cozy confines of his small but pleasant backyard. Bill was a normal child in all regards; he did well in school and had many friends, but he often enjoyed playing alone and letting his imagination entertain him in ways playing with other children did not. After about an hour, Bill suddenly felt a wave of cold wash over him. The icy chill stopped him in his tracks, and he started to shake uncontrollably. At the same time, a terrible odor filled the air around him, so foul that it made him want to vomit.

Eventually, the chill left his body and the putrid odor faded away. But Bill still felt different. He was tense, his senses on edge and weirdly attuned to the surroundings, which, while familiar, seemed a bit off to him. He walked over to the fence and looked down the alley leading to the nearby shore. The water appeared to be calling him. Images of wolves inexplicably flitted through his head, and he found himself fighting an absurd urge to take off on all fours toward the sea.

How long he remained like this he wasn't sure, but after a while he heard his mother calling for him. Her voice had never irritated him before, but now it acted like a spark that ignited a blinding, burning rage that engulfed his whole body and triggered a deep, guttural growl to emerge from his mouth. He turned toward his house, and in so doing caught his shoe on the fence post and tripped. His rage exploded. He grabbed the fence post and tore it from its concrete mooring so violently that grass and dirt were flung onto the back porch. His mother, watching from the back window, couldn't believe what she was seeing and called to her husband. Together they approached Bill, who was now swinging the heavy post around like a baseball bat. When his parents yelled for him to stop, he threw the post to the ground and then fell upon it, ripping at the still-attached wire fencing with his hands and teeth like a wild beast. Bill's father tried to pry the post from his son's grasp, but the boy resisted with the strength of three men.

Finally, his mother's sobs cut through Bill's rage-fueled frenzy and he dropped the post. He tried to appear calm, if only for his parents' sake, and for a brief moment he thought he was succeeding. But then the cold returned, and along with it the image of himself as something different, something they could never understand. He visualized himself as a wolf. Again, the unearthly growl rumbled forth from his depths, frightening his parents so much that they ran back to the house and locked the door.

Bill stood there alone in the backyard, panting like a dog, blood dribbling down his chin from cuts he incurred biting into the wire fencing. When he eventually felt the cold and the rage inside him subside for good, he made his way over to the house and knocked on the door. His parents eyed him cautiously through the window, but they could soon tell the little boy they knew was back. They threw open the door and Bill rushed into their embrace and cried. As the family ate dinner that night, they agreed that whatever it was that happened in the backyard had to have been a one-time event, a freakish accident of some sort, and something that should not be talked about again.

And for decades, it never was. Bill went on to have a normal, happy home life with his parents and siblings before moving out and finding success as a carpenter. In 1965, he married, and he and Abby went on to have three children together. By all accounts, Bill Ramsey was leading an ordinary but pleasant life, with no hint that he was anything other than the man he appeared to be. But inside, Bill struggled with many insecurities. He couldn't shake the feeling that he was hiding a terrible secret about himself, yet he couldn't put his finger on what it was. It didn't help that in the early days of his marriage, Bill was plagued by vivid dreams in which Abby was screaming at him to go away, covering her eyes, terrified, like he was some sort of monster. He would wake from the dreams panting and sometimes growling like an animal. Thankfully, in the summer of 1967, the dreams stopped and life became too busy between work and raising children to dwell on the metaphysical.

It wasn't until early 1983 that Bill Ramsey's "normal" life would start proving itself to be anything but. The first inkling that something troublesome was emerging unfolded during the previous autumn, when Bill found himself waking up in the middle of the night, going to the window, and staring at the moon as if it held some secret he needed to unlock. Sometimes as he did this, a sudden chill would sweep through his body, and he would be reminded of that awful afternoon when he was a boy. Images of wolves, unexpected and unbidden, would also flash through his mind as he looked at the bright lunar orb. *There's a need in me*, he thought to himself during these times. *But what?*

As the days passed, Bill tried his best to shake the feeling that something was wrong with him. He reminded himself that he was not an angry or violent person, as his family and friends would attest, and he had not displayed any manic episodes since the age of nine. His wife and children loved him. He was a peaceful, God-fearing man. He finally chalked up his unease to the stress of the downturned economy and resolved to relax more and obsess less.

A few months later, Bill and two of his friends, Jeremy and Scott, went out for beers after a particularly grueling weekend of work. A good time was had as they drank, laughed, and played darts, but toward the end of the evening, Bill started feeling that familiar rush of icy cold and sweat. He ducked into the restroom, and as he was washing his hands he looked in the mirror and nearly fainted. Staring back at him was the visage of a wolf. He closed his eyes and shook his head. The image was gone. Chiding himself for drinking too much, Bill rejoined his friends, who were getting ready to leave.

Sitting in the back seat with Jeremy while Scott drove, Bill was horrified at the violent thoughts flashing through his mind. Some deep, dark part of him wanted to reach over, grab Jeremy, and tear him asunder. He tried to banish the thoughts, but blinding rage suddenly overwhelmed him, and a deep, inhuman growl issued forth from the pit of his stomach.

"What the hell's wrong with you?" asked Scott from the driver's seat.

That was the last thing Bill remembered. His friends told him later that he lunged at Jeremy, assaulting him with claw-like hands and snapping teeth. Jeremy yelled for help while he tried to defend himself, but no matter how hard he pummeled Bill's head and shoulders with his fists, Bill kept up the onslaught and at one point even attempted to bite Jeremy's leg. Scott finally was able to pull the car over, and together he and Jeremy, with great effort, restrained Bill until he seemed to be himself once again. In the silence of the remaining ride home, Bill sat alone in the back seat, distraught not only over attacking his friend but also about what he feared he was becoming. *I am a wolf, with a wolf's hunger. Someday I will kill. I know I will.*

Eight months later, right before Christmas of 1983, Bill was on his way to work when he started experiencing near-debilitating chest pains. Afraid he was having a heart attack, he managed to get himself to the nearest hospital, where he was immediately wheeled into the emergency room. As nurses attended to him and prepped him for the doctor, Bill grew increasingly agitated. Not because his heart was in possible danger, but because he felt something else coming on, something that made him forget any other pain and terrified him to his core. The chill. It descended on him like an ice-soaked sheet. And from deep inside him came a rumbling sensation that started in his belly, slithered through his chest, and came roaring out of his throat.

The nurses jumped back. *How could such a noise come from any human?* Startled but still intent on doing their job, they tried gently pushing Bill back down on the gurney, but in a flash of movement, he grabbed the arm of the nearest nurse and bit down hard, drawing blood. She screamed as the other nurse swatted at Bill to make him let go. His rage exploded. He jumped from the gurney and went on a rampage within the room, throwing furniture about and roaring like a wild beast.

Within minutes, a policeman and other hospital staff arrived, shocked at seeing a snarling man pacing around on all fours when, based on the sounds they heard, they were expecting something more along the lines of a rabid dog. With the help of tranquilizers, they managed to wrestle Bill back to the gurney, all the while trying to avoid his ever-snapping teeth. The police officer present later recalled how Bill's face and eyes reminded him of something feral . . . something wolf-like.

While still sedated, Bill was taken to the Runwell Mental Hospital, where he stayed overnight. When he regained his clarity the next morning, he claimed he could remember nothing about the chaos at the emergency room. Although the doctors there recommended that Bill stay for testing and further evaluation, Bill stated he just wanted to go home and that he would make sure such an incident never happened again. His intentions may have been good, but the soon-to-come reality was frighteningly different.

On January 28, 1984, Bill was driving home after a visit with his widowed mom. The two of them had sipped tea and had a good time reminiscing about the past. Bill was feeling very relaxed, with pleasant thoughts playing in his head, when suddenly his mood changed to one of agitation and despair. A groan escaped his lips; he could feel "the change" coming over him. His body temperature dropped, his jawline tightened, and images of wolves took over his mind's eye. In a panic, he drove quickly to the one place he hoped could help him: the hospital.

Though it was the same hospital in which Bill had his last episode, the nurse who checked him in was new, and as Bill ranted on about wolves and a strange force taking him over, it was clear she thought he was either drunk or crazy. She told him to sit down while she went to get a doctor. But Bill couldn't wait, and it infuriated him that she didn't understand how urgent his condition was. Completely in the clutches of his wolf persona now, Bill curled his hands into claws and knocked the nurse across the room. Two men in nearby rooms who were patients heard the nurse's screams and ran to help. Bill easily tossed them aside and took off running down the hall.

Anyone who got in his way—doctors, nurses, patients—Bill picked up and hurled against the wall. Any furniture that got in his way met the same fate. The emergency sirens now blaring in the corridors only intensified his rage. He ran into a lounge where several doctors were having coffee. Meeting his stare, the doctors got up and slowly approached him. But Bill lashed out first, grabbing an intern by the throat and attempting to bite him. Before he could sink his teeth into the terrified man's flesh, four police officers burst into the room and formed a semi-circle around him. Bill dropped the intern and readied his escape. But there was nowhere to go, and quickly the officers were upon him.

Snarling and baring his teeth, Bill fought with an animal-like fury. He grabbed one of the officers by the hair and threw him violently to the floor, injuring him to such an extent that he had to stay in the hospital for several days. Seeing their fallen comrade, the other officers renewed their efforts, and with fists, feet, elbows, and clubs, eventually incapacitated Bill. By the time they placed handcuffs on him, the rage had faded and Bill felt normal again. Normal, but ashamed and horrified at what he had done. He knew he had gone too far this time. The Wolf Man was on his way to jail.

For over an hour, Bill was interrogated, tested for alcohol, and finally placed in a holding cell by himself. He was on the edge of despair, wondering if he'd ever see Abby again, when an officer came in who identified himself as the police surgeon. He urged Bill to tell him everything about his "seizures," no matter how bizarre things might sound. Bill resisted at first, not wanting to sound crazier than he already appeared, but finally relented and told the doctor about his lifelong struggle with wolf fantasies and losing control to some "force" that made him act like, well, a wolf. To Bill's surprise, the doctor didn't tell him he was nuts, ridicule him, or order him locked up. He did suggest that Bill voluntarily go back to Runwell, explaining that he sincerely thought the doctors there could help him. Bill told him he couldn't do that. He couldn't bear the thought of being labeled insane and losing his friends and family. To Bill's surprise, the doctor then told him he was free to go. But, he warned with a hint of anger in his eyes, the next time Bill ended up in jail, he would be going to Runwell without a choice.

It would be almost three years before the Wolf Man reappeared. On July 22, 1987, Bill stopped off at a favorite watering hole after work. One quick beer soon turned into multiples, and after a few hours, Bill was decidedly feeling the effects. Not wanting to risk getting stopped for drunk driving, he took a less-traveled route home that took him through the town's red-light district. Not surprisingly, at some point along the way Bill noticed a lone prostitute walking along the side of the road. For some inexplicable reason, upon seeing the girl, Bill came up with a bizarre plan to make a citizen's arrest. He pulled his van over and motioned for her to get in. Thinking he was a customer, the girl agreed to go with him. After a few blocks of riding in silence, she finally asked Bill where he was taking her. He told her she was too young to be a prostitute and he was taking her to the police station. She laughed nervously; something about Bill's demeanor made her uncomfortable.

When he actually pulled up in front of the station, the girl was both relieved and scared. Bill had started making low-throated growling noises and she honestly didn't think he was going to let her leave. But when she opened the door and he didn't try to stop her, she seized her opportunity and raced into the brightly lit building. She told the first policeman she saw that she was frightened of a man in the parking lot and needed protection.

Meanwhile, Bill stood outside his van, feeling oddly at peace even while "the change" was coming over him. He could feel his body respond, his hands curling into paw-like extensions, his throat rumbling with growls, his legs tightening, ready to spring. And in his mind, he saw himself running down a road, faster and faster, changing into something else as he ran. Never before had he felt such a powerful sense of himself as a wolf.

Officer Brad Busby, a big man with a reputation for being able to control any situation, approached Bill outside the station. He could tell Bill had been drinking, but there was something else about him that made Busby nervous. He tried talking to Bill but got no response, so he took him by the elbow to steer him into the station. Bill jerked away and emitted a throaty growl that Busby at first thought came from the police dog kennel nearby. But then he knew it came from Bill. And at that moment, Bill attacked.

"Before I knew what was happening, he threw me to the ground and got on top of me," Busby is quoted as saying in the book *Werewolf* by Ed and Lorraine Warren. "His face underwent an incredible transformation. His eyes got especially crazy. His lip pulled back over his teeth and his hands suddenly became claw-like. He was tearing at me the way an animal would, as if he was trying to rend my flesh."

With sheer, unimaginable strength, Bill wrapped his hands around Busby's neck and squeezed. "When the devil's in me, I'm strong!" he chanted over and over. Just as Busby was on the verge of unconsciousness, several other officers ran out and pulled Bill off their injured comrade. Roaring like a beast, Bill charged at the officers and tossed them about like they were made of straw. Six more officers came out and encircled the snarling, crouching, frenzied figure before them. They rushed at him all at once, restraining him enough for the police surgeon to inject him with a tranquilizer. That allowed them at least to drag him to a cell, but a second sedative was needed to stop Bill's attempts at biting them and, finally, to knock him out. One of the officers stated later:

"Oh, I didn't have any doubt what we were dealing with here. All you had to do was look at him. Later on, after it was all over, I was the first one to state over beers that I thought we'd been dealing with a werewolf. What surprised me was that several others agreed with me right off. No man could look or sound the way Bill Ramsey did that night. It would be impossible."

True to his word, the police surgeon had Bill committed to the Runwell Mental Hospital. Over the course of ten days, numerous tests were conducted on him, including brain scans and X-rays, as well as various psychiatric tests and evaluations. Nothing abnormal was found in any of the tests, and certainly nothing that could explain his violent outbursts. These results made Bill more depressed than ever. If there was no condition, then there could be no cure. He wasn't sure he could allow himself to live much longer with that reality.

The police station attack propelled Bill Ramsey's case into the media spotlight and soon everyone was talking about the "Southend Werewolf." Renowned demonologists and paranormal investigators Ed and Lorraine Warren happened to be in London when they first heard about it on a television show called *Incredible Sunday*. Intrigued by what sounded to them like a case of demonic possession, they reached out to the Southend-on-Sea police station and talked to Constable Kevin Berry. When pressed, Constable Berry gave his opinion that something diabolical was attached to Bill Ramsey. He also told them that while the incident with the prostitute was the story that broke headlines, there were at least two other episodes since then that had been just as horrible. The Warrens trusted Berry's assessment and asked if he could arrange for them to meet the Ramseys. A date was set.

Bill and Abby met with the Warrens at a restaurant three days later. At first, Bill understated what had been happening to him over the past few years for fear of sounding unbelievable. But with prompting from Abby and Lorraine, he finally opened up completely about the "attacks" that would overpower him, take over his body and mind, and leave him wallowing in despair. Ed became particularly interested in Bill's account of the fence post incident when he was a child and the odd coldness that had coursed through his body at that time. To some extent, Bill added, he never really felt that the chill went away; he sensed that it was always in him, lying dormant until one of the attacks came on.

After Bill finished with his story, Ed told him he was most likely possessed by a demonic spirit, a wolf spirit in this case, and would need an exorcism to get rid of it. Bill was at a loss for words. He had always thought that exorcisms were the stuff of movies and cheap paperbacks. Sensing Bill's hesitancy, Ed persisted: "I'd like you to come to the United States and meet our friend, Bishop Robert McKenna." Bill's head was spinning. First an exorcism and now traveling overseas? He told Ed that they didn't have the money to go to America.

"Don't worry about the expenses," Ed said. "We'll take care of that. We'll be here for another two weeks. Why don't you think it over?"

Bill and Abby did think it over. In fact, for the next several days, that's all they thought and talked about. Abby was all in on the idea. She was confident the exorcism could help. Bill wasn't so sure, but then something happened that left him willing to try anything.

Bill was watching television on the couch one night when he felt the familiar deep chill pass through his body and his hands begin to curl into claws. He had never had an attack at home before, and he was terrified as to what he might do. He cried out for Abby, who came running in from the kitchen. Bill flung himself down on the floor, hoping the feeling would pass quickly this time. The Ramsey's dog, Dusty, a brown and white terrier mix, started growling at Bill, but then, sensing that his owner was in pain, came over and lay down against Bill's side. Bill couldn't help himself. He snarled and then backhanded Dusty so hard that the dog flew across the room and slammed into the wall. Abby shouted, "Billy! Stop! Billy! Stop!" Over and over she kept repeating the plea. Somehow, miraculously, Abby's voice reached past the wall that usually barricaded Bill from reason and control during his episodes. After fifteen minutes, he felt back to normal. He and Abby sat on the couch holding each other, hoping and praying that Bishop McKenna could release him from this hound of hell.

Robert McKenna was a bishop in the Orthodox Roman Catholic Movement, a sect of traditional Catholicism that broke from the Church after the Second Vatican Council. Bishop McKenna was a renowned exorcist who worked with the Warrens on many cases, including the Smurl haunting case that was featured in the Fox TV movie *The Haunted*. Before introducing him to the Ramseys, Ed and Lorraine filled the bishop in on Bill's condition and backstory. After listening to the Warrens, Bishop McKenna agreed with them that Bill was most likely under the influence of a demon and that it first accosted him that Saturday afternoon in his parent's backyard when he was a boy.

Meanwhile, Bill and Abby had arrived in Connecticut along with a journalist and photographer from the British tabloid magazine *The People*, which had agreed to pay the expenses for the trip in return for story rights. Before the actual rite could begin, however, Bill was required to undergo a complete physical exam, including an EKG, to ensure he was fit enough to handle the stress of an exorcism. He passed those tests, but one more trial awaited him that night. It would be a terrible test of will, conducted by an entity that seemed to know its time was nearly up. And that wouldn't go without a fight.

Abby couldn't sleep the night before the exorcism. Too many worries and "what if" scenarios played in her head, the biggest being, what if the exorcism didn't work? What would they do then? It didn't help that Bill was sleeping fitfully beside her. He was worried too, she knew, but she was glad he was getting a bit of rest, at least. She finally started to nod off when she heard a low, feral growl coming from Bill's chest. She immediately opened her eyes and watched in horror as Bill slowly sat up, the sheet falling away from him, and turned to look at her. His eyes were the color of blood rubies and his lips were pulled back to expose impossibly large and sharp teeth. He reached for her with claw-like hands.

Abby screamed and tried to roll out of bed, but Bill was too quick. He grabbed her by her nightgown and pulled her to him. Abby fought to get free, but Bill's frenzied strength was no match for her futile actions. He got on top of her, snarling and snapping his teeth at her face. Abby knew her only chance was to speak to him like she did when he had hurt their dog.

"Bill," she said as calmly as she could. "Bill, I want you to stop this. Bill, please stop."

But unlike that evening at home, this time her words only seemed to enrage him more. He roared and wrapped his hands around her throat. As he squeezed tightly, hot spittle spraying from his mouth, Abby feared her life was nearly over. With one last reserve of strength, she thrust the heel of her palm into his jaw. The blow knocked his hands away from her neck, giving Abby an opening. She rolled off the bed and slammed onto the floor. With Bill scrambling after her on all fours like a berserk beast, she managed to crawl over to a table and grab an empty soda bottle. Wielding it above her head as a weapon against her attacking husband, Abby made one last effort to reach him. "Bill, I love you." Seeing a flicker of hesitation in his blood-red eyes, she said it again. "Bill, I love you."

He stopped advancing. Abby watched in amazement as his face lost its wolf-like appearance of only moments before and he became Bill, her Bill, once again. His coiled, tightened body relaxed and he collapsed on the floor. "Help me, Abby. Help me," he pleaded. Abby cradled him like a small child until dawn. *The exorcism had to work. It had to. Please, God.*

Bill sat in a chair facing the altar. Seated around him at Our Lady of the Rosary church were Abby, Ed and Lorraine, the journalist and photographer from *The People* newspaper, and four burly off-duty policemen whom Bishop McKenna hired as protection. The bishop himself stood next to Bill, and then, with a nod to those present, he started the rite. As Bishop McKenna read aloud the Latin prayers and exhortations from his exorcism manual, Bill felt increasingly skeptical and unimpressed. He felt nothing happening to him, even after twenty minutes or so of "mumbo jumbo," as he thought of it at the time. Thirty minutes into the ritual, Bishop McKenna pressed his stole against Bill's forehead and, taking Bill's head in his hands, ordered the wolf demon to leave. Chaos immediately ensued.

Bill began to thrash around in his chair. His face contorted into the visage of a feral animal, his eyes wild and red, and his teeth bared and sharp. Lorraine stated later that even his ears appeared more pointed. Bill would only remember that he could feel the worst attack ever coming upon him. Blistering rage shook his body to its core, and perversely violent images filled his head. Then, the wolf fully manifested and Bill became lost to its control. He lashed out at Bishop McKenna's face with his claw-like hands. Two of the policemen jumped up to grab Bill, but the bishop waved them back down. "Not yet," he said. Then Bishop McKenna took a crucifix from within his garments and held it in front of Bill's face. Bill exploded with fury. He sprung from his chair, snarling and growling, and lunged at the bishop like a rabid beast. Bishop McKenna dodged his attack and retreated behind the altar railing. Then, facing Bill, he held the cross up once again and loudly commanded the demon to leave.

Bill had been seconds away from rushing the bishop and tearing him to shreds, but as the ancient Latin words echoed in his ears and the vision of the cross impressed upon his eyes, he suddenly felt weak and shuffled over to his chair to sit down. The coldness in his body started to recede, and his desire to attack began to fade. The bishop came and stood over him while continuing to recite the words of the exorcism rite. As Bill listened to the sing-song quality of the Latin, he could feel the demon's power slipping away. It issued a faint growl from Bill's mouth and tried to move Bill to lunge at the bishop again, but Bill could simply not provide it with a physical means. All strength had left him. His eyes were closing and he was losing consciousness. But right before the blackness enveloped him, he felt a peace of soul the likes of which he had never experienced before. The wolf was gone.

Bill Ramsey had no further encounters with the wolf spirit after his exorcism. Nor did he experience any personality changes or physical seizures. He and Abby and their children went on to live a quiet and happy life in Southend-on-Sea, where the only time Bill felt the wild urge to run toward the water was when his family gleefully insisted he join them as they frolicked in the waves.

Selected Bibliography

Bitto, Robert. "The Man-Bat of Northern Mexico." *Mexico-Unexplained.com*, February 12, 2017.

Coleman, Loren. *Mothman and Other Curious Encounters*. Paraview Press, 2002.

Gerhard, Ken. *Encounters with Flying Humanoids: Mothman, Manbirds, Gargoyles & Other Winged Beasts*. Llewellyn Publications, 2013.

Hollis, Heidi. *The Hat Man: The True Story of Evil Encounters*. Level Head Publishing, 2014.

"Houston Batman Remains Mystery Decades After Reported Encounter." *abc13.com*, June 17, 2018.

"The Jersey Devil." *Fox Nation's Monsters Across America*. Aired January 19, 2021.

Leslie, Mark and Rhonda Parrish. *Haunted Hospitals: Eerie Tales About Hospitals, Sanatoriums and Other Institutions*. Dundurn Press, 2017.

Lloyd-Jones, Buster. *The Animals Came in One by One: An Autobiography*. Secker & Warburg, 1966.

Marlowe, John. *Crime Files: Chilling Case Studies of Human Depravity*. Arcturus Publishing, 2012.

McCloy, James F. and Ray Miller. *The Jersey Devil*. Middle Atlantic Press, 1976.

Offutt, Jason. *Darkness Walks: The Shadow People Among Us*. Anomalist Books, 2009.

Okonowicz, Ed. *Possessed Possessions: Haunted Antiques, Furniture and Collectibles*. Myst and Lace, 1996.

Ramsland, Katherine. "Shadow People." *PsychologyToday.com*, July 14, 2013.

Redfern, Nick. "The Glowing Winged Woman of Vietnam." *MysteriousUniverse.org*, October 23, 2015.

——. *Paranormal Parasites: The Voracious Appetites of Soul-Sucking Supernatural Entities*. Llewellyn Publications, 2021.

Ricksecker, Mike. *A Walk in the Shadows: A Complete Guide to Shadow People*. Haunted Road Media, 2020.

Roberts, C.R. "Mount Ranier-Area Youth Has Close Encounter in the Foothills." *Tacoma News Tribune*, April 24, 1994.

Sawyer, J.W. *Deliver Us From Evil*. OmniMedia Publishing, 2009.

Steiger, Brad. *Real Vampires, Night Stalkers and Creatures from the Darkside*. Visible Ink Press, 2010.

Strickler Lon. *Winged Cryptids: Humanoids, Monsters & Anomalous Creatures Casebook*. Beyond the Fray Publishing, 2021.

Swancer, Brent. "Werewolf Demons: The Bizarre Case of the Southend Werewolf." *MysteriousUniverse.org*, October 19, 2016.

Verplaetse, Jan. "Bloodlust: Where is the Scientific Evidence of a Thirst for Blood?" *ScienceFocus.com*, May 22, 2020.

Warren, Ed and Lorraine Warren. *Werewolf: A True Story of Demonic Possession*. Graymalkin Media, 2014.

Weatherly, David. *The Black Eyed Children*. Leprechaun Press, 2017.

About the Author

John Harker is a freelance journalist and ghostwriter who's been writing and publishing since the 1990s. His personal encounters with unexplainable phenomena have inspired him to explore strange, dark, and disturbing topics in both non-fiction and fiction. He lives with his family in eastern Washington, where the ghosts are dry and dusty.

Visit John's website, johnharkerbooks.com, for updates on book releases, paranormal news, and other information.

Also by John Harker

Hell Unleashed: True Tales of Possession, Oppression and Other Satanic Havoc

Demons Unleashed: True Tales of Terror Wrought by the Occult

When Demons Attack: True Tales of Diabolic Encounters

Evil Unleashed: True Tales of Spells Gone to Hell and Other Occult Disasters

Demonic Dolls: True Tales of Terrible Toys

Ouija Board Nightmares: Terrifying True Tales

Ouija Board Nightmares 2: More True Tales of Terror